1000 things you should know about

horses

1000 things you should know about

horses

Marian Curry

Miles Kelly
PUBLISHING

This material was first published as hardback in 2004

This edition published in 2007 by Miles Kelly Publishing Ltd
Bardfield Centre, Great Bardfield, Essex, CM7 4SL

2 4 6 8 10 9 7 5 3 1

Editorial Director: Belinda Gallagher
Art Director: Jo Brewer
Editorial Assistant: Bethanie Bourne
Volume Designer: Ian Paulyn
Reprographics: Anthony Cambray, Stephan Davis,
Liberty Newton, Ian Paulyn

British Library Cataloguing-in-Publication Data
A catalogue record for this book is available from the British Library

ISBN 978-1-84236-851-0

Printed in China

info@mileskelly.net
www.mileskelly.net

ACKNOWLEDGEMENTS
The publishers would like to thank the following
sources for the use of their photographs:

Cover: Jean Schweitzer/fotolia
Background images: Jürgen Hust/fotolia, John Young /fotolia
p7 (T/R) Jo Brewer, p8 (T/L) Jenny Deakin, p13 (B/R) Shires Equestrian
Products, p14 (T/L) Janice Boyd, p16 (T/L) E Jefferies and Sons Ltd,
p16 (B/L) Karl Norman, p17 (B/R) Shires Equestrian Products,
p18 (T/L) Lisa Clayden, p18 (B/L) Horseware Ireland, p19 (B/R) Shires
Equestrian Products, p20 Karl Norman, p21 (B/R) Lisa Clayden, p22 (T/L)
Lisa Clayden, p22 (B/L) Bob Langrish, p23 Shires Equestrian Products,
p25 (T/R) Bob Langrish, p26 (TB/L) Lisa Clayden, p27 (B/R) Shires
Equestrian Products, p29 (T/R) Shires Equestrian Products, p32 (T/L)
Acquire Image Media, p33 (B/R) Acquire Image Media, p35 (T/R) Acquire
Image Media, p35 (B/R) Lisa Clayden, p36 (T/L) Evergreen Hamlet,
Nicholas Pound, p36 (B/L) Inglegarth Illustrations/Townsend Aaron,
Janice Boyd, p37 (T/R) Bob Langrish, p43 (T/R) Ifor Williams Trailers Ltd,
p44 (B/L) Shires Equestrian Products, p46 (T/L) Shires Equestrian
Products, p50 (T/L) Shires Equestrian Products, p58 (B/L) Shires
Equestrian Products, p59 (B/R) Horseware Ireland, p60 (T/L) Shires
Equestrian Products, p60 (B/L) Horseware Ireland, p61 (T/R) Laurent
Laurent Vicenzotti/fotolia, (B) John Young/fotolia

All other photographs and artwork from the MKP Archives

CONTENTS

DEVELOPMENT AND ANATOMY

TACK AND EQUIPMENT

HORSECARE AND EQUIPMENT

BREEDS AND DISCIPLINES

HORSES AND PEOPLE

EQUINE FACTS AND VOCABULARY

Development of the horse

● **Fossils show that the horse's earliest ancestor** can be traced back 55 million years to *Eohippus* – a small mammal with four toes on its front feet and three on its hind feet.

● **Over millions of years**, this animal gradually developed a single hoof on each foot and longer limbs so it could move over a wide area in search of food.

● **These animals roamed in herds for safety**. As the horses travelled across the continents, the differing climates and terrain produced a different kind of horse.

● **The hotter climates** produced horses that could cope with the extreme temperatures.

● **Horses from hotter climates** were noted for their speed, while those from cooler climates were strong and calm.

● **Mongolian tribes** were first to domesticate the horse about 5000 years ago.

● **All domestic horses** in the world today are descended from these ancestors and are called *Equus caballus*.

● **For centuries**, horses have served man in agriculture and industry, as pack animals and transport, and in warfare, leisure and sport.

● **Today**, there are over 150 breeds of horse and pony.

● **Horses who do not belong to a specific breed** can be categorized into types, such as hunter or cob.

▼ *The gradual evolution of the horse.*

Eohippus   Mesohippus   Parahippus   Merychippus   Pliohippus   Equus

Relatives of the horse

● **Horses belong to the *Equus* family**, as do zebras, mules and donkeys. *Equus* comes from the ancient Greek word meaning 'quickness'.

● **There are three species of zebra** and they are all found in southern Africa. Each species lives in a different habitat and has its own patterns of stripes.

● **Zebras are highly gregarious animals**, congregating in large groups.

● **Female donkeys carry their foals** for 12 months before they are born – two months longer than a female horse.

● **The Quagga**, a variety of zebra, became extinct in the 19th century.

● **Donkeys were first domesticated** about 6000 years ago and are still used as work animals. They can carry heavy loads over long distances on little food or water.

● **The feet of donkeys**, like horses, grow continuously and need to be trimmed about every six weeks.

● **'Jack' is the name** given to the male donkey, 'jennet' to the female.

● **A mule is a hybrid** of a horse and a male donkey. A hinny is a cross between a female donkey and a horse.

● **Mules are well-known** for their strength and good temperament, but they can be stubborn.

▼ *Donkeys can live for as long as 30 or 40 years.*

Horse sense

● **The senses**, sight, hearing, smell and touch are much more highly developed in horses than in humans.

● **Horses respond to touch all over the body** – especially on their ears. They can sense a fly landing on any part of their body and use their tail to flick it off.

● **A horse's eyes are set apart** on either side of its head. It has a good view of its surroundings – except directly in front of its nose and directly behind its tail.

● **Horses have large ears** that rotate 180 degrees.

● **The ears of a horse can indicate** how it is feeling. If they are laid back flat it is feeling aggressive.

● **Using smell alone**, horses are able to recognize humans and animals they are familiar with.

● **Horses are also sensitive** to smells in their environment, such as dung, dirty troughs, musty feed, bad water and certain plants.

● **The whiskers that grow from a horse's muzzle** and around its eyes are used to feel objects around them and should never be removed.

● **When a horse is cold**, it will feel cold to the touch behind its ears.

● **Horses have a good long-term memory**. A horse will often remember where it got a fright and will continually shy at that place.

▼ *Most horses have four natural gaits: walk, trot, canter and gallop.*

▼ This horse appears relaxed. Its ears show no sign of tension.

★ STAR FACT ★
Horses are attracted to sugar. Like humans, they will often reject sour, bitter and unusual tastes.

Conformation

- **Different breeds of horses** are defined by the size or shape of their body (conformation). They should be symmetrical and balanced.

- **A horse's head** should be in proportion with its body.

- **The feet should be neat** and the front and back pairs should be symmetrical.

- **Eyes should be large and clear.** They should not show large patches of white.

- **The back and hindquarters** should be strong and well muscled. The back should not be too long for the horse's height as this could result in weakness.

- **A parrot mouth is where a horse has an overbite,** the top teeth overhang the bottom teeth.

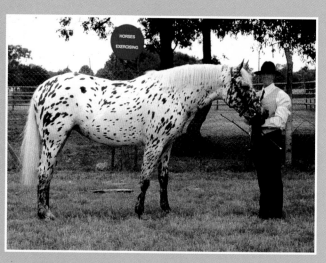
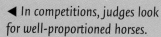

◀ *In competitions, judges look for well-proportioned horses.*

- **Cow hocks mean the feet turn inwards.** Bow legs mean the feet turn outwards.

- **A sway or hollow back,** is where the horse's back dips from the withers showing a prominent backbone.

- **A ewe neck** makes a horse look as though its neck is on upside down, with the strong muscles underneath rather than on top.

- **Flat feet may be the result of low heels.** A horse with this condition can find it painful walking over rough ground, which can lead to bruising and lameness.

Vital parts

- **Horses guard their personal space.** This is about 4 m around themselves. Only friends, horse or human, are allowed to come closer.

- **An adult horse's brain** weighs about 650 g – about half the weight of an adult human brain.

- **A horse usually has** 54 vertebrae in their backbone. Arab horses are the exception, having slightly fewer.

- **When galloping,** a horse supports all its weight on one hoof. It takes nine months to one year to grow a completely new hoof.

- **Native ponies** usually choose to keep their droppings in distinct areas to keep the maximum amount of pasture for grazing.

- **A horse's skeleton** is divided into two main sections: the axial skeleton – the skull, spine, ribcage and pelvis, and the appendicular skeleton – the bones of the limbs.

- **At rest,** a horse breathes between 10 and 15 times a minute.

- **Blood makes up about 8 to 10 percent** of a horse's total body weight.

- **Standing still,** a horse's pulse measures 46 to 42 beats per minute. If frightened this can rise quickly to over 250.

- **Horses have 16 muscles** in each ear, enabling them to detect sound coming from any direction.

▶ *A galloping racehorse can reach speeds of up to 70 km/h.*

Feet

- **Horses are odd-toed animals,** having only one toe or hoof on each leg.

- **Domestic horses** usually need to have their hooves trimmed about every six weeks.

- **Horses that work** or travel on hard roads need their hooves protected by metal shoes. These need to be replaced every 4 to 6 weeks.

- **The person who cares for a horse's feet** is called a farrier.

- **To measure a horse's or pony's foot for shoes,** take the measurement across the widest part of the foot and also from the toe to the heel.

- **Hooves are made of keratin,** a protein that is the same substance as human hair and nails.

- **The frog is the rubbery wedge-shaped part** on the underside of a horse's hoof. It helps absorb shock as the hoof hits the ground, and prevents slipping.

> ★ STAR FACT ★
> Horseshoes are considered lucky and replicas are often carried by brides on their wedding day.

- **Mud can absorb moisture** from the hoof wall and make it brittle.

- **A horse often** paws the ground as a sign of frustration.

Remedial shoes for foot problems

Traditional hind shoe

Traditional front shoe

▲ Different styles of horseshoe can be fitted to suit the needs of the horse.

Height

- **Horses are measured in hands.** One hand is equal to 10 cm.

- **A hand measurement** was originally based on the width of a man's palm and was later standardized as 10 cm.

- **The measurement** is taken from the ground up to the withers, the highest point on a horse's shoulder.

- **For an official measurement,** the horse has to have its shoes removed.

- **Below the height** of 14.2 hh, horses are classed as ponies. However, sometimes this rule does not apply.

- **An Arab is always called a horse** even if it is only 14 hh, and polo ponies are always called ponies even if they are 15 hh.

- **Falabellas are the smallest breed** in the world, measuring around 76 cm. They are good-tempered and friendly.

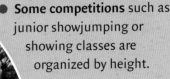

> ★ STAR FACT ★
> The tallest horse was a Shire called Samson. He measured just over 21.2 hands (219 cm).

- **Some competitions** such as junior showjumping or showing classes are organized by height.

- **Height is not the only difference** between horses and ponies. Ponies usually have different conformation and may have a bouncier stride.

◀ Small breeds of pony are often measured in inches or centimetres.

Markings

- **Markings are areas** of white on a horse's body.

- **The clumps of hair** growing at the back of the fetlocks are called feathers.

- **Some breeds have very fine, short hair** while others, such as Shire horses, are famed for their long, thick feathers.

▼ *White leg markings are described by using the points of anatomy that the white hair covers.*

Coronet   Fetlock   Stocking

★ STAR FACT ★
Some horse breeds still show primitive leg stripes and dorsal stripes along their backs.

- **Horses have chestnuts** – horny plaques that grow on the inside of each of their legs.

- **A snip is a small area** of white above the top lip or around the mouth.

- **A prophet's mark** is a small dimple on the horse's skin, usually found around the neck or shoulder. It is thought to be lucky.

- **Some white hair growths** are not natural markings. They are the result of old injuries.

- **Ermine marks are dark spots** on top of markings just above a hoof.

- **Pink-skinned horses** can suffer from sunburn, particularly on areas where their hair is fine or thin, such as the muzzle.

- **Horses can be security marked on their skin**, usually by freeze marking under the saddle area or on the neck under the mane.

Coats and colours

- **Horses can be either one colour** all over (whole colours) or a mixture of colours (broken colours).

- **The most common whole colours** are bay, black, brown, chestnut, dun, cream, palomino and grey. The broken colours include piebald, skewbald, roan and spotted horses.

- **Horses that work during the winter** are often clipped to remove their thick winter coats to keep them cool while working.

- **Piebald and skewbald** have coats made up of patches of either black and white, or white and another colour, usually brown.

- **Strawberry roan and blue roan** describe a mix of chestnut and grey, and black and grey hairs.

- **Light or dark bay** is brown with a dark mane and tail. The amount of dark or light hair in the coat determines which type of bay.

- **Chestnut horses** vary from reddish brown through to deep reddish gold.

- **Spotted horses** have grey coats spotted with black or brown.

- **All white horses** are called greys.

- **A palomino** is a light gold colour with a light mane and tail.

▼ *A team of chestnut-coloured horses, showing variation in mane colour and face markings.*

Stallions and geldings

- **A stallion is a male horse** capable of siring foals.

- **A gelding is a castrated** or gelded male.

- **Male horses reach maturity** at about two years, but they are known as colts until they are four years old.

- **In the wild**, two-year-old colts are driven off by the stallion to form their own bachelor groups.

- **The stallion in charge** of a group of mares will round them up and fight off any advances by rival stallions.

- **Domestic stallions** are usually kept away from both mares and geldings.

- **Stallions require special handling** and need experienced owners, so they do not become over dominant and difficult to handle.

- **Horses are gelded** from the age of about six months, so they cannot reproduce.

- **Geldings are usually more dependable** and tolerant than other horses.

- **If mares and geldings** are kept together they may fight for dominance, each trying to be the leader of the group.

▼ In the wild, stallions will normally have about four or five mares.

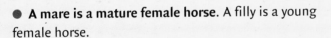

Mares

- **A mare is a mature female horse.** A filly is a young female horse.

- **Mares are pregnant**, or 'in foal', for 11 months. Most give birth to a single baby called a foal.

- **A mother (dam)** recognizes her foal by smell. She spends the first hour after birth licking and sniffing her foal to create a bond between them.

- **Mares produce milk** for their young and will feed them for up to six months before they are weaned.

- **During foaling**, mares need peace and quiet. Disturbing them may cause their labour to stop.

- **Mares should not** normally be ridden after they are five months pregnant.

★ STAR FACT ★
Some mares reject their foals. The foals can sometimes be raised by a foster mare.

- **A mare is said to be in season** – receptive to a stallion and fertile – for about five days in every 21-day cycle.

- **Mares mainly come into season** when the days are longest and warmest – from early spring until late autumn.

- **Although a mare becomes** less fertile with age, she can often continue to produce offspring into her late teens.

- **Mares in season can be** more sensitive than geldings. During this time they require sensitive handling.

◄ A pregnant mare needs more food than usual.

Foals

- **When foals are born** their legs are almost the same length as when they are fully grown.

- **Spring is the usual time** for foals to be born, as the weather improves and grass is at its most nutritious for mares.

- **Foals can focus their eyes** almost as soon as they are born. Within an hour they can stand up and walk.

- **Within a day** a foal can gallop to keep up with its mother.

- **A newborn foal** will often kick out if touched on its quarters by an animal other than its mother.

- **Young foals have very long legs** in relation to their body. As they develop, their body proportions balance out.

- **Foals tend to sleep** flat on the ground rather than standing up.

- **In the wild**, filly foals may stay with their mother for several years as part of a family group. Foals like to play, and enjoy chasing and grooming each other.

- **Within a week a foal will have cut its first teeth**, and will have a full set of teeth by about nine months.

- **Foals start on solids**, picking at grass, or investigating their mother's feed buckets, from six weeks. They should be wormed for the first time at this stage.

- **After its first birthday** a foal is called a yearling. By three to four years of age ther are fully grown.

▶ A mare will continue to suckle a foal until it is about six months old. By this time the foal will be eating a variety of other foodstuffs and be ready for weaning.

Herds

- **Horses are social animals**, preferring to live in family groups that join together into herds.

- **A herd is usually led by a mare** who decides when the group should move on to look for fresh grazing.

- **One horse in the herd** will always be on guard. If it senses danger, it will alert the others and the herd will gallop away.

- **Horses can gallop at 48 km/h.** However, they are not designed to gallop for prolonged periods of time.

▶ *Horses will groom and nuzzle one another.*

- **When there is danger**, foals are moved to the centre of the group and protected by the adults.

- **Horses can communicate** with other members of the herd through both vocal and body signals.

- **Fighting is uncommon**, as horses show their displeasure by lashing their tails, flattening their ears or striking out with their front legs.

- **Domestic animals** often lack the company of an entire herd and can feel vulnerable.

- **It is important** to offer a horse some company, if not another horse then a donkey or sheep.

- **When a horse dies**, the remaining horse will often grieve for its missing friend and can show signs of depression.

> ★ STAR FACT ★
> In the wild, horses spend up to 70 percent of their time grazing.

Teeth

▶ *Different types of teeth are used in eating. The surface of the teeth is worn down by about 3 mm every year.*

Large, broad-topped molars are used to grind plants and vegetation

Premolars start to break down the food

Incisors used to tear plants from the trees and ground

- **A foal has a set of milk (baby) teeth**. These are worn down as it begins to graze, and are replaced by the adult (permanent) teeth.

- **A horse's teeth** continue to grow upwards from the root throughout its life.

- **By the age of five**, a horse will have all its permanent teeth.

- **Horses have upper and lower incisors**, so they can nip grass very short.

- **In old age**, from about 20 onwards, a horse will begin to lose its molar teeth.

- **The maximum** number of teeth an adult male horse has is 44.

- **The vet files down** the teeth to ensure there are no sharp edges to the teeth, which could be painful.

- **Some horses dislike dental treatment** and have to be sedated.

- **The best way to discover** the age of a horse is to examine its teeth. Vets can also tell a horse's age from changes and marks on the teeth.

- **A very old horse** will have short molars. A molar might only be 3 cm long compared to 8 cm in a young horse.

Body facts

- **On average**, a horse's stomach can hold 9 to 12 l. Food passes through the digestive system quickly.

- **Horses can suffer from cracked lips**. The sides of their mouths should be inspected regularly.

- **Horses need to eat a lot of fibre**, such as grass and hay. They need to consume about 2.5 percent of their bodyweight in dry matter each day.

- **Some ponies don't know when to stop eating**. This can cause colic and laminitis if their pasture is too lush.

- **Oils, such as vegetable**, soya or linseed can be added to a horse's feed to help improve its coat condition and add extra calories to the diet.

- **After feeding**, horses produce manure. In a healthy horse, this should break softly when it hits the ground – being neither hard pellets nor liquid manure.

- **A horse drinks** at least 25 l of water each day – about 13 times as much as an adult human.

▶ On average, a horse at grass eats for 15 out of every 24 hours.

★ STAR FACT ★
The oldest horse on record is Old Billy, who died in November 1822 at the age of 62.

- **The Flehmen response** is a particular way of smelling that involves the horse turning out its upper lip and extending his nose in the air.

- **A horse** cannot vomit.

Poisons

▶ Horses could develop oak poisoning after eating acorns and oak leaves, which could be fatal.

- **Horses can easily poison** themselves with the natural vegetation found in their fields, or in the trees and hedges surrounding their paddocks.

- **Care should be taken** to ensure that poisonous plants are removed from within their reach.

- **Paddocks must be inspected** weekly as new seeds may germinate after the parent plant has been removed. A ragwort plant can produce 150,000 seeds.

- **All parts of yew** can cause immediate death if ingested.

- **It is estimated** that a large number of horses and ponies die from ragwort poisoning in Britain every year.

★ STAR FACT ★
Horses should never be fed mown grass as it can cause serious colic.

- **Eating ragwort**, a yellow flowering weed, affects the liver and can result in death.

- **The tree** *Laburnum vossii* has poisonous seeds and leaves that can leave a horse in a coma if eaten.

- **If poisoned by eating bracken**, a horse will grow increasingly sleepy and arch its back.

- **Even the common buttercup**, is mildly poisonous and can cause mouth irritation. However, when dried in hay, it is quite safe.

- **Both acorns and oak leaves** are poisonous to horses. In the autumn, acorns and leaves should be removed in case they are blown into areas where horses graze.

Points and condition

- **A horse's body parts** are identified through a series of points.

- **Condition refers to** a horse's outward appearance. A shiny coat, clear eyes, clean nose and ribs that can be felt but not seen, are all indicators of good condition.

- **Worms that live** in a horse's system are parasites. If left undisturbed, they result in loss of condition and in cases of severe infestation, colic.

- **Regular worming** throughout the year is essential in domestic horses to keep infestation under control.

- **Laminitis is a painful foot condition** which restricts the blood flow to the feet. An affected horse will often place its weight on its heels to relieve the pain.

- **It is necessary** to study a horse's behaviour in relation to other horses, as well as its interaction with humans. This determines whether it is generally a quiet, dependable sort or an independent flighty animal.

- **Hocks are joints** on a horse's hind legs.

- **The withers should be the highest point on** a horse's back. They are found at the base of the mane.

- **Heels are found on the underside** of a horse's foot. A farrier must take care when shoeing that the shoe does not impinge on the heel, causing corns.

- **Fetlock joints are found on all four legs**. They are below the horse's knee on its front legs and below the hocks on its back legs.

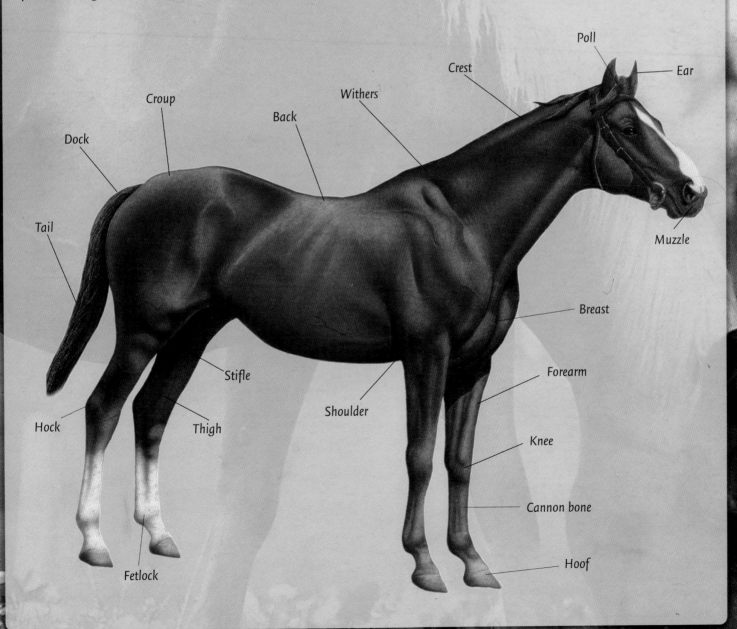

Saddles

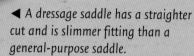

- **A well-fitting saddle** carries the rider in the correct position without causing the horse any discomfort.

- **Traditionally made from leather**, lighter synthetic saddles are now popular.

- **Saddles come in a number** of different styles, such as pony, jumping, dressage and general-purpose.

- **Saddles should be cleaned** and checked regularly to ensure there are no lumps underneath the seat that could damage the horse's back.

- **When buying a new saddle**, an experienced saddle fitter should fit one that is appropriate for both horse and rider.

◄ A dressage saddle has a straighter cut and is slimmer fitting than a general-purpose saddle.

- **The fit of a saddle** should be reassessed regularly to fit the horse.

- **Numnahs are saddle-shaped pads** that sit underneath the saddle to protect the horse's back.

- **Girths secure a saddle** on the horse and come in various materials and designs.

- **Stirrup leathers are the two leather loops** suspended from a saddle that hold the metal foot rest – the stirrups – to support the rider's feet.

- **Stirrup irons should be big enough** to allow about 1 cm of clearance each side of the rider's boot.

> **★ STAR FACT ★**
> The Selle Royale saddle was developed in the 17th century. This saddle is still used by the Cadre Noir in France today.

Bridles

- **A bridle is used to control** a horse's movement and direction by means of communication with its head, mouth and nose.

- **Most bridles are made of leather** but also come in different materials that can be easily cleaned.

- **Bridles come in three basic sizes**: pony, cob and full size.

- **A snaffle bridle consists of several pieces**: a headpiece, a throatlash, two cheek pieces, a brow band, a nose band, a pair of reins and a snaffle bit.

- **A bit is part of a bridle** that fits into a horse's mouth.

- **Bits are made from different materials**, including metal and rubber, and in various sizes.

- **A correctly sized bit** should show 0.5 cm either side of the horse's mouth to ensure it does not pinch its lips.

- **Some bridles are bitless**, such as the hackamore, and work by adding pressure on a horse's nose.

- **Well-maintained saddlery** is vital for the comfort and safety of horse and rider and will help to ensure that the tack lasts.

- **Sometimes a 2 cm strip** of mane is removed to allow the bridle headpiece to fit tidily behind the ears.

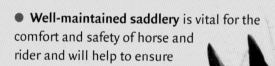

► The simplest form of bridle is called a snaffle.

Western tack

- **Saddles used in western-style riding** are heavier than normal saddles with a broader seat. They are designed to be comfortable over long distances.

- **Western saddles** were developed from the Spanish style saddles.

- **The high horn** on western saddles was traditionally used as an aid for roping cattle.

- **Western bridle reins** are usually split into two distinct pieces. Each separate piece is held in one hand.

- **The large western-type stirrups** are traditionally made from wood encased in leather.

- **The stirrup leathers** on a western saddle are called fenders.

- **The famous American** actor John Wayne presented Queen Elizabeth II with the saddle he used in the making of the film, *The Alamo*.

- **Saddle blankets are used to protect** the horse's back. Cowboys often used them as bed rolls while cattle ranching.

- **The western-style bridle** may have loops over either one or both ears and does not usually have a nose band.

- **The saddles are made from leather.** The show saddles are highly ornate, decorated with silver and heavily patterned leather.

◀ *The western saddle is geared to the needs of the rider.*

Grooming kit

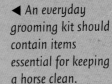

- **Every horse should have its own grooming kit** that is kept solely for its own use. This prevents infectious skin conditions being passed to other animals.

- **The basic kit consists of brushes**, sponges, a hoof pick and a means of cleaning the brushes. It is important to regularly remove dirt, hair and old skin matter.

- **The dandy brush has long, stiff bristles** and is used to remove dried mud and dirt from a horse's winter coat.

- **The body brush is softer** and is used to remove grease and dust from a horse's summer coat. It can be used on sensitive areas.

- **A water brush** is used for applying water to the horse's coat, mane and tail when dampening or washing.

- **A rubber or plastic curry comb** is used to remove dried mud and loose hair from the coat.

◀ *An everyday grooming kit should contain items essential for keeping a horse clean.*

- **A metal curry comb** should never be used on a horse but is used to remove dust and dirt from the brushes.

- **Hoof picks** are used for removing dirt and stones packed into the underside of a horse's hoof.

- **Stable sponges** are used for cleaning the eyes, nose, nuzzle and tail area.

- **Grooming should be done** outside so that dust is not inhaled. A lightweight plastic container or a canvas bag with a drawstring top makes an excellent storage for a grooming kit.

First-aid kit

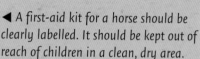
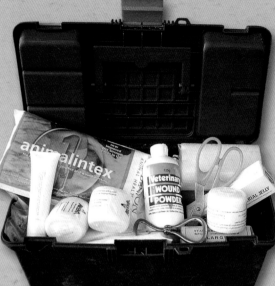

- **Every horseowner** should have a first-aid kit, but a vet must always be called if there is any doubt as to the severity of an injury.

- **A basic kit should contain** commercial poulticing material that can draw out impurities from a wound, such as an abscess in the foot.

- **Wadding is useful to remove** dirt and to absorb blood from an injury.

- **A rubber boot** is a useful item and helps protect an injury.

- **Elastic bandages for holding a poultice** in place are essential, but care must be taken when applying wraps to ensure they are not tied too tightly.

◀ *A first-aid kit for a horse should be clearly labelled. It should be kept out of reach of children in a clean, dry area.*

- **Access to cold water**, disinfected containers, sharp, clean scissors and unused sponges should also be part of a basic kit.

- **A suitable antiseptic** and a barrier cream to soothe sore skin and heels should be included.

- **Wound powder or gel** is needed for minor abrasions.

- **A pair of tweezers** is useful in case a thorn or splinter has to be removed from an injury.

- **Cool gel packs** can be used on swollen or strained areas to reduce inflammation.

Rugs

- **Domesticated horses** require protection against the elements.

- **Each horse should have at least** two rugs in case one is damaged or wet.

- **The most basic rug** is one which simply keeps the rain off.

- **Fine-coated horses**, or those that have been clipped, need rugs that offer warmth as well as being waterproof.

- **Stable rugs** provide warmth indoors but are not water-repellent.

- **Wicking rugs**, which allow moisture to escape, are useful in drying a horse that is wet from rain or sweat.

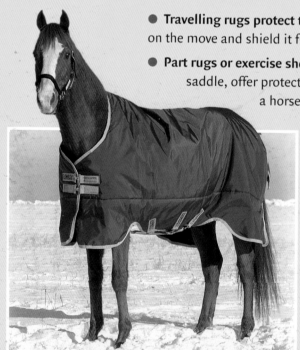
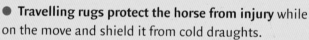

- **Travelling rugs protect the horse from injury** while on the move and shield it from cold draughts.

- **Part rugs or exercise sheets**, which sit behind the saddle, offer protection from the weather while a horse is exercising.

- **Rugs should be checked** at least twice a day to ensure they are not rubbing the horse.

- **Before storing**, rugs need to be cleaned and mended to keep them in good condition.

◀ *A rug may be needed to protect a horse from the weather.*

Travelling equipment

● **Travelling in a horsebox or trailer** is an unnatural experience for a horse and every effort should be made to make the journey as stress-free as possible.

● **The horse should wear safety equipment** to help prevent any injury during loading, unloading or travelling.

● **When leading a horse into a trailer or horsebox**, an appropriately sized headcollar and travelling rope should be used.

● **An anxious horse** may throw its head up high, so it is important to protect the vunerable poll area.

▶ *The owner should familiarize the horse with the trailer or horsebox.*

● **Travelling boots fitted to each leg** protect against injury. In addition, knee and hock defenders can be worn for extra protection.

● **A rug is used to protect the horse** from draughts while travelling.

● **A tail guard protects the tail** during travelling.

● **The person loading the horse** should wear gloves in case the leading rope is unexpectedly pulled through their hands.

● **If a haynet is used while travelling**, it must be secured at a height where the horse cannot entangle itself in the net.

● **Any unsecured items** must be removed before setting off as these may move around and frighten or injure the animal.

Rider wear

▶ *An approved safety hat should always be worn for horseriding.*

● **Most riding schools are** happy to provide safety hats for beginners.

● **Riding clothes are designed** to give the rider protection in the event of an accident.

● **Jodhpurs or breeches** are comfortable and practical and protect the legs from being pinched or chaffed from stirrup leathers.

● **A body protector provides protection** for the back, neck and shoulders.

● **Short or full-length leather boots** with a clearly defined heel give ankle support and prevent a rider's foot slipping through the stirrup.

● **Wellington boots** should not be worn for riding as they may get caught in the stirrups.

● **Fluorescent vests**, called tabards, help make riders more visible to road users.

● **Gloves are essential**, both to keep hands warm and to prevent the reins being pulled out of a rider's hands.

● **Long hair should be tied back** to prevent it getting tangled or obscuring the rider's view.

● **Earrings or any other form of jewellery** should be removed before riding.

● **Riders wishing to take part in competitive riding**, such as showing, jumping or cross-country, will find there are dress codes for each discipline that must be adhered to.

Road safety

● **When riding on roads** safety issues are very important for both horse, rider and other road users.

● **If possible, riders should travel** with another rider, or a friend on a bicycle or walking alongside.

● **A young or inexperienced horse** should never be ridden on the road until it has proved itself in a controlled situation.

● **Riders should wear high-visibility** clothing to allow drivers the earliest chance of seeing them and driving with caution.

▲ *Even during the summer months when visibility is generally good, a rider wearing a fluorescent tabard helps drivers to see them.*

▲ *Horse and rider should be well prepared and wear suitable equipment for travelling on the road.*

● **A riding hat that meets current** safety standards should always be worn, together with a body protector.

● **Observation is one of the keys** to road safety. The rider should keep away from busy main roads and be alert to moving traffic, continually looking and listening for hazards that may alarm the horse.

● **Riders should give clear and accurate signals** to inform other road users where they are going.

● **Parked vehicles should be given** sufficient berth to allow a passenger to open a door without injuring the horse or rider.

● **Riders should inform someone** of their planned route and the time it will take them to complete it, so an alarm can be raised if they fail to return.

● **A mobile phone should be carried** in order to call for help in the event of an emergency. Phones should be switched to silent mode while riding to avoid startling the horse with a ringing tone.

Happy and relaxed

● **A relaxed horse allows its head and neck** to hang low when at rest. A tense or anxious horse has its head held high.

● **A happy horse may make chewing or licking** movements with its mouth. This shows it is happy to do what its owner says.

● **An excited or nervous horse** is ready to run off at any moment. A calm horse's walk will be unhurried.

● **A tense horse will have a rapid pulse** – a rider may be able to feel its heart beating. A relaxed horse may sigh or yawn and take deep breaths.

● **The skin should be soft and supple**, not stretched taut over the muscles.

● **The lips should be soft and relaxed**. The mouth should not be tight or pinched.

● **Eyes should be large and clear**. The membranes under the eyelids and linings of the nostrils should be salmon-pink in colour.

● **A happy horse can be touched** all over and will show no sign of irritation, such as tail swishing.

● **The horse should offer up a foot** to be cleaned without hesitation on command. By freely giving a foot, the horse shows trust in its carer.

● **If a horse sees** a familiar person in its field, it will call out and approach, showing it is happy to be with them.

◄ *An alert expression denotes a healthy and happy horse.*

Feeds and feeding

● **Horses have small stomachs** and need to eat little and often. If kept in a field, horses will graze for most of the day.

● **Feed is one of the main costs** of keeping horses. However, feeding horses well-balanced diets is also the principal way of keeping horses healthy.

● **There are many different foodstuffs**: concentrates, forage, supplements, vitamins, and herbs. Roughage must play the largest part in their diet.

◄ *Succulents, such as apples and carrots, can be added to a feed to make it more appetizing.*

● **It is essential to provide a balanced diet** that contains correct levels of vitamins and minerals.

● **Proprietary balanced feeds** offer a consistent diet and are convenient to use. They are carefully formulated to meet the requirements of different types of horses.

● **All concentrates should be kept** in rodent-proof containers to avoid attracting vermin and wasting food.

● **Hay should be stored off the ground** in a dry, ventilated area.

● **Before purchase**, hay should be inspected to guarantee it is free from ragwort. It should not appear dusty, smell bad or have any visible mould.

● **Sudden changes in the type of food** can cause digestive upset.

● **Clean water must be available** at all times – either from a self-filling container or from a trough.

Common ailments

▶ Mud *fever affects a horse's heels and lower legs and shows as sore, reddened, scabbed skin.*

● **COPD (chronic obstructive pulmonary disorder)** is an allergy caused by dust or mould spores. It affects a horse's breathing and results in a cough or nasal discharge.

● **Thrush affects** the underside of the hoof. It is often caused by unhygienic bedding or standing in wet, muddy conditions.

● **An abscess on the sole of the foot** can cause lameness in a horse. It is caused by a small cut that gets infected.

● **Ear mites cause irritation** – an affected horse might shake its head and try to scratch its ears. The condition can be treated with creams.

● **Aural plaques** are wart-like flakes in the ears and are usually harmless.

● **Colic is abdominal pain** – it can usually be detected if a horse is looking agitated and uncomfortable.

● **Lice live on horses**, causing bald patches as the horse tries to itch the affected areas. Louse powders and shampoos are used to treat the problem.

● **Mud fever is usually caused** by standing in wet and muddy fields. Bacteria enters the softened skin around the legs and needs to be treated with special anti-bacterial washes and creams.

● **Laminitis is inflammation** of the sensitive laminae in a horse's foot. It is likely to occur if a pony grazes for too long on overly lush or fresh grass.

Worming

● **All horses have some parasites** in their stomach and intestines.

● **Small quantities of parasites** will barely effect the horse. Danger arises when the parasite count builds up.

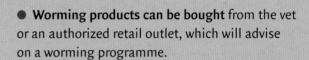

● **A badly infested horse** may look thin, and have bouts of anaemia or colic.

● **There are several types** of worm found in horses: red worms, tapeworms, lungworm, pin worms, round worms and bots.

◀ *Paste wormers come in a syringe which is squeezed onto the horse's tongue.*

● **Worming products can be bought** from the vet or an authorized retail outlet, which will advise on a worming programme.

● **Most horses should be wormed** every eight to ten weeks. All horses living together should be wormed at the same time.

● **Horses who are new to a paddock** should be wormed and kept apart from other horses for 48 to 72 hours, the amount of time it takes for food to pass through their system.

● **All droppings should be removed from fields**, at least two or three times a week, and should be stored on a muck heap. The contents of a muck heap should not be spread over horse pasture.

● **Grazing horses with sheep and cattle** helps to keep worm levels down. The larvae do not affect sheep and cattle and die in their stomachs.

● **Wormers come in liquid**, powder and paste forms.

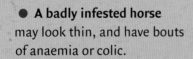

Horseshoes

● **People have protected horses' feet** with shoes for over 2000 years.

● **A horse's feet should be cleaned out** twice a day to ensure there are no stones, sticks or mud trapped under the foot that could lead to lameness.

● **Not all horseshoes are nailed on.** In special circumstances, plastic shoes can be glued on.

● **Racehorses wear special lightweight shoes** made of aluminium rather than the typical iron shoe. These are called racing plates.

● **Today, farriers in Britain** have to undergo a four-year apprenticeship to qualify as a registered farrier.

● **Farriers have been part of an organization** in Britain since 1356, when the Worshipful Company of Farriers was formed.

★ STAR FACT ★
The Romans used a type of iron sandal on their horses' feet.

● **A farrier's job is highly skilled.** It requires knowledge not only of how to make and put on shoes, but also of the horse's movement and diseases of the foot.

● **Shoes can be fitted** by the farrier at the forge, or the farrier can to travel to clients with a portable forge.

● **Special hardened studs** are sometimes added to shoes for better grip. There are types of stud for different ground conditions and disciplines.

▶ A hoof pick for cleaning horses' feet is a vital piece of equipment for every horseowner.

▲ After removing an old set of shoes, a farrier has to trim and balance the horse's feet prior to re-shoeing.

▶ The pointed end of the anvil allows the farrier to shape a shoe to the correct size.

Buying a horse

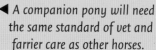

● **Before purchase**, it is important to find out as much as possible about the horse's history. A responsible seller should be able to provide veterinary and worming records.

● **It is important to consider** the horse's age, size, temperament and conformation.

● **All horses and ponies** should be vetted prior to purchase by an equine veterinary surgeon.

● **Blood tests and X-rays** can also be part of the vetting procedure.

● **Horses take time to settle** into new homes and may show untypical behaviour for the first weeks after a move.

● **Horses require twice-daily attention** and year-round care. Anyone considering the purchase of a horse must be fully aware of the costs and time involved.

◄ *A companion pony will need the same standard of vet and farrier care as other horses.*

● **The purchase price** is only a small part of the cost of keeping the horse, which will include grazing, stabling, vetting, feeding, worming, tack and insurance.

● **Horses are herd animals** and thrive on company.

● **When buying a horse**, it is worth providing it with a companion.

● **Before buying a horse**, determine whether the price includes tack and equipment.

Stabling

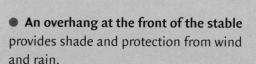

▶ *The stable door should be high enough for the horse to easily walk through without banging its head.*

● **Stables are used** to shelter a horse from the extremes of weather.

● **An average-sized stable** is 3.7 x 3.7 m.

● **A stable should be built** with its back to the prevailing wind, on level ground and with an area of hard standing to the front.

● **The stable and its doors** should be of adequate height so the horse does not bang its head.

● **Stables must have good ventilation** to ensure the air inside does not become stale.

● **An overhang at the front of the stable** provides shade and protection from wind and rain.

● **The floor of the stable** should be non-slippery and hard-wearing. Concrete with rubber matting is often used as it can be washed down and disinfected easily.

● **The doorway should be wide enough** to allow the horse to pass through it comfortably.

● **Stables should be cleaned out** regularly, and droppings and wet material removed daily.

● **Horses kept in stables** for long periods without any form of exercise can develop behavioural problems such as weaving, crib-biting, windsucking and box walking.

Field shelters and barns

● **All horses and ponies need field shelter.** They not only require protection from the cold, wet and windy weather, but need shade during the summer.

● **Field shelters are usually open-fronted sheds** that may house several horses in the paddock.

● **Horses should have as much free time** in the company of other horses as possible.

● **Shelters may be sited directly onto the earth** but still require to be cleaned of droppings regularly.

● **Mobile field shelters** are designed to allow for movement between paddocks.

● **Horses can share** a large barn at night or in bad weather.

● **Communal living** means that horses don't get lonely and can stand together for comfort and warmth.

● **One of the disadvantages** of allowing several horses to share a field shelter or barn is that infection can spread quickly and a newcomer might be picked on by others.

● **A horse with a dust allergy** may be unsuitable for communal living. If it has to have dust-free bedding it will need separate accommodation.

▼ *A field shelter or open barn offers protection from the elements.*

Paddocks

▶ *Turnout headcollars are designed to pull free if the horse becomes caught on fencing.*

● **Domesticated horses** have a limited area of grass in which to eat, play, and leave their droppings.

● **Each horse needs** about 1 to 1.5 acres for grazing.

● **A horse's carer must remove droppings regularly,** check for and remove any poisonous plants and fill in any holes a horse could stumble into.

● **The border fencing and hedging** around a paddock must be well maintained to ensure horses cannot escape or injure themselves.

● **In spring and early summer,** and again in the late autumn, it might be necessary to restrict grazing, as lush grazing could result in laminitis or colic.

● **If enough grazing is available,** it is a good idea to divide it into smaller sections. This allows one area to be grazed while the other sections rest.

● **A wet field can result in** horses developing ailments such as mud fever or thrush.

● **Good maintenance of the gates** is necessary to ensure the horse is not in danger from sharp edges or broken panels.

● **Horses should always have access to fresh water.** A trough should be provided in the field that can be checked daily and topped up as necessary.

Hints and tips

- **Vet bills can be very expensive.** It is therefore important to be aware of your horse's condition and to take action before any problems develop.

- **Insurance policies are available** to cover third-party liability, loss-of-use and veterinary treatment and costs.

- **Share the responsibility of horse care** with other horseowners, so that you can look after each other's horses rather than having to pay someone else to do it.

- **Savings can often be made** by buying large quantities of various products.

- **Develop a routine for essential daily chores** to save time and energy.

- **Be prepared to be flexible** in your choice of horse rugs and equipment.

- **Try to source your hay and straw locally,** so that you do not have to pay large delivery charges.

- **Keep a spare pair of trousers and boots** in the tack room so clothes do not get dirty when visiting a horse in its field.

- **Book regular appointments** with the farrier for re-shoeing every six weeks.

- **Take rugs to be cleaned and repaired** as soon as winter is over in order to keep them in good condition.

▶ To help avoid mud fever, make an area of hardstanding at gateways.

Horse whispering

- **Horse whispering** has moved from folklore to established practice.

- **People now understand** it is a means of communicating in the way a horse naturally understands.

- **Horses communicate** with each other through minor visual and audio signs.

- **By understanding a horse better,** the trainer can work out how best to deal with it.

- **If a horse is approached** square on it will see this as confrontational, and may flee.

▶ Horses often form a strong relationship with another horse they live with – this is called pair-bonding.

- **Horses move each other on** by walking behind another horse's flanks and possibly nudging them with their noses.

- **Although they are often scared,** horses can be trained not to run away, to trust their carer and to accept that they will not be put in any real danger.

- **Many horse communicators** use special halters. These make it easier for the handler to teach the horse the difference between acceptable and unacceptable behaviour.

- **Monty Roberts** is a leading US exponent of horse whispering and has done much to establish it around the world.

The healthy horse

▶ A healthy horse will appear relaxed and content in the paddock.

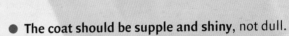

● **When looking after a horse**, it is important to be aware of what is 'normal' for the individual. If a horse is behaving unusually, its carer is quickly aware of the situation and can act promptly.

● **A healthy horse has bright clear eyes**, which are not weeping or discharging. The ears should be alert, not drooping or uninterested or held tightly back.

● **Respiration at rest** should be between 10 to 20 inhalations per minute.

● **A horse's pulse rate** is normally 35 to 45 heart beats a minute at rest.

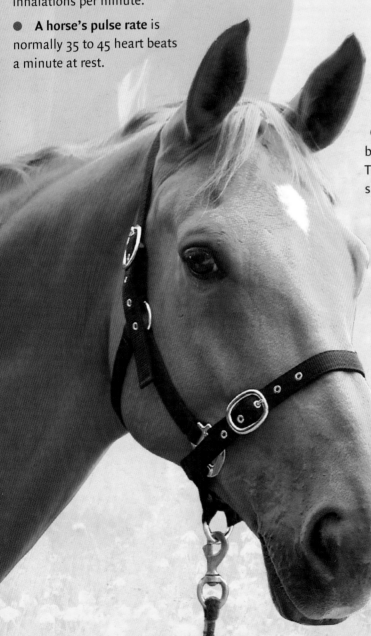

● **The coat should be supple and shiny**, not dull.

● **The normal temperature** of a horse is 37.5 to 38.5 °C.

● **A healthy horse supports its weight** on all four feet equally and shows no sign of swelling in its feet or legs.

● **The sounds coming from a horse's stomach** should be 'normal' for that individual and not particularly loud. The stomach should not be distended and the horse should be eating and drinking normally.

● **The tail should be relaxed** and not clamped down between the horse's back legs.

● **A horse should not stand** in a depressed manner at the back of its stable or away from companions in the paddock. Any signs of irritable or untypical behaviour may indicate the horse is feeling unwell.

● **Healthy horses have a good appetite**. Loss of appetite is the first sign of health problems.

◀ By taking a good look at its demeanour and expression you can tell a lot about a horse's health. An interested expression suggests the horse is not unwell or in distress.

Behavioural problems

- **Behavioural problems or vices** can be the result of stress or boredom.

- **If a horse is confined in a stable alone** over long periods of time, it will become unhappy and will often develop unwelcome habits.

- **One solution may be** to turn out the horse for longer periods in the company of other horses.

- **Weaving is when a horse stands** at an open stable door repeatedly swinging its head.

- **Boxwalking** is where the horse refuses to settle and walks repeatedly around the confines of its stable.

- **If a horse shows reluctance** to be saddled, the saddle should be checked immediately.

- **Windsucking is similar to crib-biting** – the horse attaches its teeth to a piece of wood and sucks in air.

- **A horse may buck** if the saddle is causing it pain – the saddle should be checked immediately.

- **If a horse begins to headshake**, it may have a tooth problem and a horse dentist should examine it.

- **Crib-biting** is the habit of biting or chewing wood.

- **The rider may benefit** from further riding lessons so they are not putting themselves or the horse in any danger.

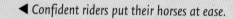

◀ *Confident riders put their horses at ease.*

Daily routine

- **Horses enjoy routine** and expect to be fed at roughly the same time every day.

- **A horse should be visited every morning** to check it is safe and well.

- **During the morning visit,** the horse should be fed, its feet picked out and any rugs adjusted. Plenty of fresh water should always be available in the stable or field.

- **Manure should be removed from the field**. The stable or shelter should be cleaned and prepared for the evening.

- **A horse should be ridden** at least an hour after feeding to allow it time to digest its food.

- **Grooming after exercise** is relaxing for the horse.

- **After riding**, a horse should have its feet picked out again and its rug replaced, if necessary, before being returned to its field or stable.

- **In the evening,** the horse should be brought back inside if stabled, or checked again in the field.

- **The feed buckets should be cleaned out** ready for the next feed.

- **The food and bedding supplies** should be checked and reordered regularly. The worming and vaccination programme should also be checked to ensure it is being adhered to.

◀ *Rugs should be added or removed according to daily conditions.*

Grooming

- **A carer should wear gloves**, sturdy boots and, if necessary, a riding hat.

- **A headcollar and leading rope** should be put on the horse before bringing it out of its stable or field.

- **The horse should be tied up** using a slip knot that can be easily undone if necessary.

- **Any rugs should be removed**. If it is very cold, rugs can be turned over on themselves, leaving only a part of the horse's body exposed. This is known as quartering.

- **Grooming should begin** with picking out the feet.

- **The next stage is to remove any mud or dirt** from the horse's coat. Care should be taken not to overgroom, as natural grease in a horse's coat helps to keep it warm and dry.

- **The face should be cleaned** using a soft brush and sponge. It is best to untie the horse while cleaning this area, holding onto the leading rope with one hand.

◄ *Grooming stimulates circulation and helps keep the coat and skin clean and healthy.*

- **Particular care should be taken** to thoroughly groom the areas where tack sits.

- **Brushes should be cleaned** repeatedly against a metal curry comb during the course of grooming.

- **A thorough grooming removes dirt from the coat** and makes the horse look clean and shiny. Once the neck and body are finished, including the legs, the mane and tail should be carefully brushed out.

- **While grooming never sit or kneel down** next to the horse. Always squat, in case the horse is startled and moves suddenly.

Tacking up

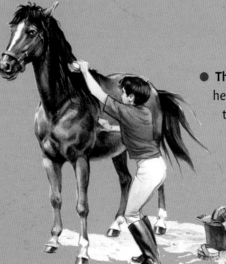

▶ *The horse should be thouroughly groomed before and after being ridden.*

- **A horse should be clean** prior to being tacked up and should be approached in a calm manner.

- **The underside of the saddle**, numnah or saddlecloth should be checked to ensure there are no sharp objects or insects.

- **The rider should stand on the horse's left-hand side**. The saddle should be positioned on top of the numnah and slid back into the correct place.

- **The saddle should sit far enough back** to allow free movement of the horse's shoulders.

- **The rider should walk around the front of the horse** to drop the girth down from the saddle, then return to the left-hand side to fasten the girth so that the saddle is secure.

- **The bridle is placed** on the horse's head from the left. The reins are then passed over the head.

- **The bit is placed** into the horse's mouth by inserting a thumb into the gap in the teeth, which helps to open the mouth.

- **The headpiece is fitted over the ears**, the throatlash fastened and the noseband done up. Check that no pieces of the bridle have been tangled.

- **The rider should then recheck the girth** and tighten if necessary.

- **Horses should not be left tacked up** for any length of time as they might try to roll.

Learning to ride

- **Riding schools should be checked out** by visiting them rather than simply booking a lesson by telephone.

- **A new rider** is **taught the basics** – controlling speed, turning and stopping and good balance.

- **Beginners are provided with riding hats.** They will be introduced to a suitably sized, calm mount and shown how to get onto the horse.

- **The first lesson** will probably be conducted on a leading rein with an adult walking alongside the horse.

- **The rider will be taught** how to approach a horse correctly, how to mount and dismount, sit correctly and how to hold the reins.

- **A new rider will learn** the basics of balance and stability in the saddle, so that they do not injure the horse's mouth or back.

- **Canter should be introduced later** when the rider has a confident seat and is able to control the speed and direction of the horse.

- **Children usually enjoy** the company and competitiveness of group lessons.

- **Jumping is taught** when the rider is proficient at all the basics.

◀ *Rising trot lets the rider feel the movement of the horse and 'post' or rise in time with the stride.*

Complementary therapy

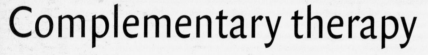

- **A vet should be consulted** before any complementary treatment is sought.

- **Osteopaths and chiropractors** work to reduce pain and increase mobility by manipulating the horse with their hands.

- **Physiotherapists may incorporate** other means such as hydrotherapy and ultrasound.

- **Hydrotherapy involves specially designed tanks** in which horses can swim to improve their muscles and build up fitness.

- **Acupuncture uses special acupuncture needles** on points around the body. The aim is to restore an animal's health by correcting its energy flow.

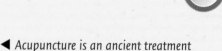

◀ *Acupuncture is an ancient treatment used for a variety of common ailments.*

- **Equine sports massage** encourages a faster recovery after muscle damage and is frequently used on competition horses.

- **Holistic vets** use aromatherapy and homeopathy to treat animals.

- **Shiatsu is a form of massage** that is said to help both a horse's physical and mental state.

- **A more controversial therapy** is distance healing. This usually involves sending a piece of horse's mane or tail to a healer who does not actually visit the horse, but thinks about it from a distance.

Welfare organizations

- **All domestic animals** deserve to be well-treated.

- **Equine welfare organizations** work towards protecting all horses, ponies and donkeys.

- **The International League for the Protection of Horses** (ILPH) was set up in England in 1927 by Ada Cole. The main aim was to 'prevent the ill-treatment of horses exported to Europe for slaughter'.

- **The ILPH** is now one of the world's leading equine welfare charities.

- **In Britain**, the ILPH has four rehabilitation and recovery centres caring for about 300 horses.

- **In Britain and the USA**, there is legislation to protect horses. If someone is convicted of a serious offence against a horse they can be sent to prison and fined.

- **Farriers are bound by laws** that aim to ensure horses are not subjected to unnecessary suffering by being shod by unskilled people.

- **The British Horse Society** is the UK's largest equine charity, aiming to improve the welfare of horses and ponies and promote the interests of its member horseowners and riders.

- **The Donkey Sanctuary in England** was set up 30 years ago by Dr Elisabeth Svendsen and has cared for almost 9000 donkeys.

- **The International Donkey Protection Trust** works worldwide to improve conditions for working donkeys and mules in Europe, Africa, Egypt, India and Mexico.

▲ International charities and organizations work worldwide to protect the best interests of horses, donkeys and mules.

▶ Welfare charities offer support and advice for owners and can take action if animals are poorly treated.

Arab

- **The Arabian horse**, or Arab, is the oldest pure-bred horse in the world.

- **The Arab was the horse of the Bedouin people** – nomadic Arabs – as early as 3000 to 2500 BC.

- **This ancient breed is widely regarded** as the definition of beauty and elegance in horses.

- **Famed for its speed**, strength, and endurance, the Arab has influenced the development of most modern horse breeds.

- **Arabs usually stand** 14 hh to 15.2 hh.

◄ The Arab has a small head, large eyes, and a thin muzzle.

> **★ STAR FACT ★**
> The anatomy of the Arab horse is unique –
> it has 17 ribs, one less than other breeds.

- **Arabs are intelligent**, sensitive, courageous creatures. They are also loyal, if well-treated, and enjoy attention.

- **Some Arabs that carried their famous riders** into battle were Napoleon's Marengo, Alexander the Great's Bucephalus, and the Duke of Wellington's Copenhagen.

- **The earliest Arab horse** brought to the US was a stallion called Ranger, which arrived in 1765.

- **The action of the Arab is unique** and the breed is characterized by a 'floating' movement – covering the maximum amount of ground with the minimum of effort.

- **During the Crimean War** (1851–54), an Arab horse galloped 150 km without harm, however its rider died from exhaustion.

Quarter Horse

- **The Quarter Horse was bred to race short distances** – no more than a quarter of a mile. It is the oldest all-American breed.

- **Quarter Horses measure between** 14 hh to 16 hh. They are mainly chestnut.

- **Powerful and muscular conformation** gives the Quarter Horse speed, ability and balance.

- **The breed was developed** by English colonists in the early 1600s.

- **Known for its 'cow sense'** – the ability to out-manoeuvre cattle – and calm disposition, the Quarter Horse was ideally suited for the challenge of the West.

◄ Quarter Horses are used in western riding competitions, demonstrations and rodeo.

- **The breed is renowned** for its versatility and excellent temperament.

- **The Quarter Horses** is North America's favourite breed with over two million listed by the American Quarter Horse Association.

- **The American Quarter Horse Association** was formed in 1940.

- **The agility and speed of the Quarter Horse** makes it ideal for ranch work.

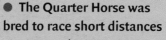

Thoroughbred

- **The Thoroughbred** stands 15 hh to 16.2 hh.

- **The history of the Thoroughbred** and the birth of the racing industry are interlinked.

- **The introduction of Arab blood** increased the speed and endurance of the breed. Thoroughbreds are now the most famous racehorses in the world.

- **Racing is called 'The Sport of Kings'** because the English kings of the 15th century encouraged the development of racing and breeding of Thoroughbreds.

- **The first Thoroughbred** arrived in America in 1730.

▶ Thoroughbred racing is a popular sport.

> ★ STAR FACT ★
> Thoroughbreds can begin their racing career at just two years old.

- **Thoroughbreds are usually** whole colours. Many have white markings.

- **Three famous stallions**, Byerley Turk, the Darley Arabian and the Godolphin Arab are seen as the founders of the Thoroughbred breed.

- **Thoroughbreds are unsuitable for** inexperienced riders because they can be temperamental and may overreact to surprises.

- **Horses that retire** from the racing industry require careful rehabilitation and re-homing.

Shire and Clydesdale

- **The Shire originated in England** and is a descendant of the Old English Black Horse.

- **The Shire stands** up to 18 hh, and may be bay, brown, black or grey.

- **Shires still work the land** in some parts of Britain and several brewers use them to pull drays in the city streets.

- **The Shire Horse Society** was founded in 1878 to 'promote the old English breed of cart horse'.

- **Shire numbers dropped** after World War II but today there is a renewed interest in the breed.

- **Clydesdales are a breed of heavy draught horse**, recognized for their strength, style, and versatility. The breed originated from Scottish farm horses.

◀ The mane and tails of Clydesdale horses are ornately decorated for

- **Clydesdales worked** on farms and transported goods within and between towns.

- **The ability to pull** many times more than their own weight made the breed popular for transporting goods by wagon.

- **Growing to over 18 hh**, Clydesdales are usually bay or brown in colour with four white legs and a mass of soft feathers about the feet.

- **The Clydesdale was the first draught horse** in Great Britain to have an individual society. The Clydesdale Horse Society was founded in 1877.

Welsh Ponies and Cobs

● **The Welsh breed** is split into four sections: A, B, C and D.

● **The original and smallest of the Welsh breeds** is the Welsh Mountain Pony (Section A). It stands no more than 12 hh and is most commonly grey – although it can be any colour except piebald and skewbald.

● **The Welsh Mountain Pony** should have a small head with neat pointed ears, big bold eyes and a wide forehead.

● **Section B is the Welsh Pony.** These ponies were used by farmers to herd sheep and other ponies. Today the breed is mainly used as riding ponies for children. They are shown and ridden in jumping competitions.

● **Section C is the Welsh Pony or Cob type.** This pony is stronger than the Welsh Pony and was originally used for farm work. A versatile breed, it is ideal for both for riding and driving.

> ★ **STAR FACT** ★
> Welsh Ponies have been bred in the Welsh mountains since before Roman times.

● **Section D is the Welsh Cob** and the tallest of the breed. These cobs are noted for courage and endurance and are strong and agile.

● **The Welsh Ponies and Cobs** (Section B, C and D) have the same colouring as the Welsh Mountain Pony (Section A).

● **The Welsh Section B and C** do not exceed 13.2 hh. The Welsh Section D cobs will exceed 13.2 hh.

● **Welsh Ponies and Cobs** are renowned for being sure-footed, hardy and natural jumpers.

● **The Welsh Pony and Cob Society** was established in 1901 and published the first volume of the Welsh Stud Book in 1902.

▼ *The Welsh Cob makes an excellent driving pony.*

Highland and Shetland

- **The Shetland and Highland pony breeds** both originate from the far north of the British Isles.

- **The Shetland is the smallest** British native pony. It is not taller than 42 in.

- **Shetlands were originally used** as working ponies carrying peat and seaweed.

- **There are miniature** Shetland Ponies that should not exceed 34 in height.

- **Shetland Ponies** can be of any colour except spotted.

- **The Shetland is an extremely strong pony**, and is thought to be the strongest of all breeds for its size.

- **There have been Shetland Ponies** on the Shetland Islands for over 2000 years.

- **The Highland is the largest** of the Scottish breeds, standing between 12 hh and 14 hh.

- **There are two types of Highland Pony:** the Mainland, which is larger, and the smaller Island Pony.

- **Highland Ponies are a variety of colours** including dun, brown, bay and black.

- **Crofters used Highland Ponies** for haulage and farm work, and they are still used on many hunting estates to transport deer and game.

- **Highland Ponies are used** for trekking, riding for the disabled and as all-round family ponies.

◄ *Shetland Ponies are popular for showing and as children's ponies.*

Dartmoor and Exmoor

- **The Dartmoor is a small pony** no bigger than 12.2 hh and is usually coloured black, bay or brown.

- **This ancient breed** is native to Dartmoor in Devon, England.

- **Dartmoor is an exposed area of moorland** standing over 300 m above sea level. This means that Dartmoor Ponies are hardy, sure-footed animals that can survive on limited grazing.

- **Dartmoor Ponies are calm** making them suitable for children to ride and look after.

- **As well as being used on farms**, Dartmoor Ponies have been used to transport tin from the mines.

- **The Exmoor Pony has inhabited** the Exmoor moorland of southwest Britain for many years.

- **They are brown, bay or dun coloured** with lighter mealy-coloured markings around their eyes and muzzles. They stand at about 12 hh.

★ **STAR FACT** ★
Until the 1960s, Dartmoor Ponies were used to escort inmates from the local prison whilst on outside duties.

- **Exmoor ponies are thought to have existed** since prehistoric times, but are now a very rare breed.

- **In the past**, farmers used Exmoor Ponies for agricultural work and shepherding.

▶ *Exmoor Ponies have 'toad' eyes. This means their eyes are hooded.*

Connemara and New Forest

- **The Connemara is the only native pony of Ireland.** They are usually grey, black, brown or dun and occasionally roan, chestnut or palomino, measuring between 13 hh and 14.2 hh.

- **Connemara Ponies** are used today as children's ponies, and for competing, driving and showing.

- **Intelligent and willing,** Connemaras are also agile and obedient.

- **Hardy, athletic and with good balance,** the Connemara is also strong and free-moving.

▶ The Connemara makes an excellent competition pony for teenagers or small adults.

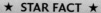

- **The Connemara breed** is often crossed with a Thoroughbred to make successful competition horses.

- **The New Forest Pony comes from southern England.** They are usually bay, brown or grey, standing 12 hh to 14.2 hh and make excellent riding ponies.

- **The New Forest Breeding and Cattle Society** produced its first stud book in 1960. The breed rules permit any colour except piebald, skewbald or blue-eyed cream.

- **New Forest Ponies** are naturally sure-footed and hardy.

- **A long smooth stride** makes New Forest Ponies comfortable to ride and they are ideal for trekking and endurance.

Fell and Dales

- **Fell and Dales pony breeds originated** in the north of England. The two breeds are genetically related.

- **Dales Ponies on average stand between** 13.2 hh and 14.2 hh. They are mostly black, but there are also bays and a few greys.

- **In the 19th century,** Dales Ponies were used for agricultural work and to carry lead from mines to the ports.

- **Often used as trekking ponies,** Dales Ponies are capable of carrying adults.

- **The Dales Pony almost became extinct** in the 1950s, but numbers increased after the formation of the Dales Pony Society in 1963.

- **Traditionally used as pack ponies,** Fell Ponies carried lead from the mines. They were also used for pulling carts and trotting races.

- **Fell Ponies vary in height between** 13 hh and 14 hh.

- **The Fell Pony has a long mane and tail,** and silky feathering on its legs.

- **An old breed,** Fell Ponies date back to Roman times when they were used as draught animals.

- **Fell Ponies are renowned for their good paces.** Their active walk and fast trot makes them an ideal driving pony.

◀ The constitution of the Fell Pony is said to be 'as hard as iron'.

Akhal-Teke

- **The Akhal-Teke is an ancient breed** that dates back over 3000 years.

- **The breed originated from the Turkoman Steppes** in Central Asia and takes its name from a nomadic tribe known as Teke found at the Akhal oasis.

- **The average height is between** 14.2 hh and 15.2 hh and an Akhal-Teke may be dun, bay, chestnut, grey or black with a short and silky tail.

- **The head of an Akhal-Teke** is similar to an Arab's and its body is described as one of the most elegant in the horse world.

- **The breed is noted for** stamina and endurance.

- **In 1935 a group of Akhal-Teke horses** were taken on a three-day trek across the desert to Moscow without water.

> ★ STAR FACT ★
> The Akhal-Teke has been used as a racehorse for over 3000 years

- **Developed to suit desert conditions** the Akhal-Teke horse has fine skin with a long back and narrow quarters.

- **In history, Akhal-Teke** have been prized by Alexander the Great, Genghis Khan and Marco Polo.

- **Turkmenistan's** national emblem features the breed.

- **The rider of an Akhal-Teke** needs to be confident and calm as they are known to have sensitive natures and to dislike strangers.

◄ *This herd of Akhal-Teke horses shows the wide range of colours common to the breed.*

Haflinger and Icelandic

- **At 13.1 hh to 14.2 hh,** the Haflinger is palomino or chestnut with a light-coloured mane and tail.

- **The Haflinger is a small, strong pony.** It has a slightly dished face and large eyes, and enjoys exercise.

- **Haflingers make good riding ponies,** and are a popular breed with centres for disabled riders because of their honest, calm natures.

- **As an established breed around the world,** there is a register of pure-bred Haflinger stallions that has been kept for over 100 years.

- **As there is no word for pony** in Icelandic, a pony under 13.2 hh, is always referred to as a horse.

- **Icelandic horses have three layers** to their coats to help them withstand the harsh climate in which they live.

> ★ STAR FACT ★
> In Italy in 2003 the first cloned horse was born to a Haflinger mare.

- **The Icelandic breed** is long-lived, and an animal is not considered mature until seven years old.

- **Icelandic horses can be any colour,** have a stocky build and are noted for good eyesight and tough nature.

- **The horses still play** a **large part in Icelandic life.** As well as being excellent family riding horses, they compete in showing, endurance, and special race meetings.

◄ *Haflingers are small and strong. They are a hardy breed ideally suited to working on mountain slopes.*

Appaloosa and Dutch Warmblood

- **The Appaloosa is an ancient breed** known for its spotted coat that comes in a variety of recognized patterns.

- **The main patterns are known as blanket**, spots, leopard, snowflake and frost. They often have black-and-white markings on their feet.

- **They have short manes and tails** and usually stand between 14.2 hh and 16 hh.

- **Appaloosas were developed by the Nez Perce** – Native American Indians who lived in north-west America.

- **Appaloosas are prized** for endurance riding, because of their strength and strong limbs.

★ STAR FACT ★
All Appaloosa foals are born with light coats that eventually grow darker.

- **The breed was virtually destroyed** in the late 1800s when the US army captured the Nez Perce Indians and killed their horses.

- **Originating in Holland**, the Dutch Warmbloods usually stand between 15.2 hh and 17 hh.

- **Dutch Warmbloods** are usually chestnut, bay, black or grey with white markings on the face and legs.

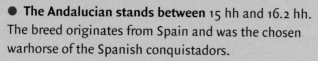

▶ Over 500,000 Appaloosas are registered in the Appaloosa Horse Club today.

Andalucian and Lipizzaner

- **The Andalucian stands between** 15 hh and 16.2 hh. The breed originates from Spain and was the chosen warhorse of the Spanish conquistadors.

- **Andalucian coats are usually grey or black**, but can also be dun and palomino.

- **The Andalucian breed is** noted for its intelligence, beauty and sensitivity.

- **In medieval times**, Andalucian horses were bred and protected by Carthusian monks.

- **The Spanish Riding School of Vienna** – the oldest riding school in the world uses Lipizzaners.

- **Lipizzaners are taught special movements** involving controlled athletic jumps and kicks called 'airs above ground'.

- **Lipizzaners usually have grey coats**. The foals are born black or brown and develop their grey coats as they mature. This can take as long as ten years.

- **Dating back to AD 800**, the Lipizzaners are a result of crossing Berber horses from North Africa with horses used by the Romans for chariot racing known as Karst horses.

- **In Spain**, Andalucians are called *purs espagnol* or 'pure Spanish horses'.

- **One of the most famous movements** performed by the Lipizzaner during displays is the levade, where it takes its weight on the hind quarters in a controlled manner while raising the upper body and tucking in its front legs.

◀ A Lipizzaner demonstrating the levade.

Tennessee Walking Horse and Morgan

● **The Tennessee Walking** breed has a particular gait that resembles a running walk.

● **They range in size** from 15 hh to 17 hh and come in a variety of colours, including black, bay or chestnut.

● **With long tails that are high set** and a deep muscular chest, Tennessee Walking Horses are said to be particularly calm and good-natured horses.

● **The first horse to develop the gliding walk** was born in 1837. This trait was developed by farmers and plantation owners in Tennessee who wanted a horse capable of covering long distances with a smooth stride.

● **Some Tennessee Walking Horses** are said to click their teeth in time to the rhythm of the walk.

● **It has become so popular** that it is one of the top ten breeds recognized in the US.

● **The Morgan originates** from Vermont in the US and dates back to the 18th century. The breed can be traced back to one stallion who took its name from its owner, Justin Morgan.

● **On average Morgans stand between** 14.1 hh and 15.2 hh. They are primarily brown, bay, black or chestnut.

● **The eyes should be large and prominent** and its shapely ears set wide apart. Mares often have longer ears than stallions.

● **The breed is noted for strength** and a particularly gentle temperament.

● **The Morgan Horse Club** was founded in 1909 to stop the decline in the breed. Today, it competes in many disciplines including showing, dressage, jumping and driving.

▶ *Morgans are popular ridden showhorses.*

Cleveland Bay and Hanoverian

- **The Cleveland Bay is the oldest breed** of English horse. It takes its name from the area where it was originally bred.

- **Standing between** 15.3 hh and 17 hh, the Cleveland Bay is bay coloured as the name suggests.

- **Intelligent** with good temperament, Cleveland Bays were popular carriage horses.

- **British royalty uses** Cleveland Bays to pull state coaches.

- **The Cleveland Bay is often crossed** with the Thoroughbred – the resulting animal makes an excellent competition horse.

- **The Hanoverian originates from Germany.** A tall horse – 16 hh to 17 hh, it may be any solid colour.

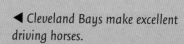

> ★ STAR FACT ★
> It is believed Cleveland Bays evolved from the horses left in Britain by the Romans.

- **The excellent gaits of the Hanoverian** include a ground covering walk, a free-moving trot and a rhythmic canter.

- **Originally Hanoverians were bred** for the military and as strong carriage horses. They are noted for their strong backs.

- **Hanoverians are now bred** as performance horses and often win at Olympic level in showjumping and dressage.

◀ *Cleveland Bays make excellent driving horses.*

Mustang, Paint and Pinto

- **The word Mustang** is derived from a Spanish word meaning 'stray' or 'ownerless'.

- **Mustang horses were introduced to the US** around the 1700s by Spanish settlers. They formed huge herds that numbered about two million by 1900.

- **In order to protect grassland grazing for cattle**, the Mustangs were culled. They are now a protected breed and their numbers are managed.

- **Mustangs stand between** 13 hh and 16 hh and can be any colour.

- **They were used by both** the Native American Indians and cowboys.

- **American Paint Horses** are clearly defined by both coat patterning and conformation. Their coats are a mixture of white and any other colour.

- **There are three recognized coat patterns** for Paint Horses called Tobiano, Overo and Tovero. The patterns relate to how markings cover the horse's body and legs.

▶ *The Pinto horse was first introduced into North America by Spanish explorers.*

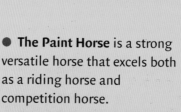

- **The Paint Horse** is a strong versatile horse that excels both as a riding horse and competition horse.

- **The Pinto horse was associated with** the North American Indians and was believed to have special magical powers in battle.

- **The Pinto Horse Association of America** recognizes different breeds and cross-breeds as long as they have the required colouring.

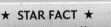

Other pony breeds

- **Przewalski's Horse is a small stubborn breed**, between 12 hh and 14 hh, dun coloured with a dorsal stripe along the back and zebra stripes on the legs. It has an erect mane and dark brown tail.

- **Camargue Ponies originate from Southern France.** Many still live in wild herds on salt marshes in the Camargue region.

- **The rare Eriskay Pony is an ancient breed** found on the island of Eriskay in the Hebrides, off Scotland. These hardy ponies were originally used by crofters to carry peat and seaweed.

- **Chinoteagues are the only pony native to the US**. They stand about 12 hh and are extremely hardy, able to survive on very little vegetation.

> ★ STAR FACT ★
> Camargue Ponies are usually grey and are known as the 'white horse of the sea'.

- **The Fjord Pony was used in battle by the Vikings**. They are striking-looking ponies, standing 14 hh to 14.2 hh, dun coloured with a dorsal stripe.

- **The Hackney is a showy, high-stepping horse or pony.** The pony stands under 14 hh – the horse 14 hh to 16 hh.

- **The Caspian is one of the oldest equine breeds**. These small ponies stand up to 12 hh and are bold and fast-moving.

◄ *The extravagant action of the Hackney makes him unsuitable as a riding pony, but excellent as a driving pony.*

Other horse breeds

▶ *Percherons have broad chests with strong forearms and excellent feet.*

- **The Brabant is descended from** the medieval heavy war horse. It is the most popular draught breed in the US.

- **The Trakehner stands between** 16 hh and 16.2 hh and can be any colour. The breed originates from Prussia.

- **The Percheron is a strong,** heavyweight horse, standing 15 hh to 17 hh. Originating from France, it has developed into one of the strongest draught horses in the world.

- **The Yili from China is a new breed**, developed from crossing Russian horses with native stock.

- **Due to their excellent stamina**, the Yili can cover long distances.

- **The Canadian Horse is renowned for its stamina**, versatility and willingness to please. Because of their hardiness, they became known as the 'little iron horse'.

- **They are usually black,** standing 14 hh to 16 hh and have docile characters.

- **American Saddlebred horses** usually stand at around 16 hh. They are popular riding and driving horses.

- **The Falabella is the best-known miniature horse breed**. It is usually about 76 cm tall at the withers.

- **The versatile Selle Français** is over 16 hh and is successful as an all-round competition horse.

Western riding

● **Western riding is not confined to America** and is popular worldwide.

● **Developed by the cowboys** in the United States, Western riding was brought to the Americas by the Spanish.

● **Unlike English-style riders**, western riders do not always wear protective headgear. The traditional head gear is a Stetson hat. Riders may also wear decorated leather cowboy boots.

● **Western riders use their weight** and neck reining to influence their horse's speed and direction.

● **By holding the reins in one hand** western-style riders have one hand free. This enabled cowboys to hold a rope when catching livestock.

▶ *The Stetson typifies the western cowboy.*

● **Reining has developed to competition level** – riders carry out a set of movements and are judged on their accuracy and the obedience of their horse.

● **On dismounting**, the western-style rider removes his right leg from the stirrup, swings his leg over the saddle and then steps down with his left leg.

● **In western riding**, the canter is called a lope and the trot is known as a jog.

● **The rodeo developed from ranch riding** and includes skills, such as saddle-bronco riding, bareback-bronco riding and bull riding. There are also timed events involving roping, barrel racing and steer wrestling.

> ★ STAR FACT ★
> The Stetson was named after John Batterson Stetson – the inventor of the cowboy hat.

Horse racing

● **Horse racing is a worldwide sport.** One of the most popular forms of the race is over flat ground.

● **Horse racing became a popular sport** during the 18th and 19th centuries when many of Britain's famous horse races were created, such as the Grand National in 1839.

● **Steeplechases were originally run** from one church steeple to another. Any fences or walls in between had to be jumped.

● **The Kentucky Derby** is the most famous horse race in America and has been held since 1875.

> ★ STAR FACT ★
> The Dubai World Cup is the world's richest horse race with a prize fund of $6 million.

● **Horse racing was illegal** in England between 1649 and 1658 when the country was controlled by Oliver Cromwell.

● **Saddles designed for flat racing** can weigh as little as 0.2 kg.

● **Point-to-point** is a race over jumps for amateur jockeys. Their mount has to have hunted at least seven times in the past season.

● **Before motorized transport**, racehorses had to walk to race meetings. They had to set off weeks before the race to give them time to recover.

● **Jockeys race in 'silks'.** These are a coloured hat cover and jacket that identify the horse's owner.

◀ *The Curragh is the headquarters of flat racing in Ireland and can trace its history back to chariot racing.*

Horse shows

- **Horse shows allow horseowners** to compete against other similar horses and ponies.

- **Classes are held for specific breeds** and types and for all levels of rider.

- **Before the show**, the horse is groomed and the tack cleaned.

- **The show and classes chosen** should be appropriate for the level of the horse and rider.

- **The day before the show**, every effort should be made to ensure the horse looks its best.

- **Tail plaiting should be done** on the morning of the show.

- **Equipment needed for a show includes**: feed and water, a grooming kit, a first-aid kit, tack, and the rider's clothing.

- **The morning of a show**, the horse should be fed and dressed appropriately for travelling.

- **Enough time should be allowed** for a calm loading and relaxed drive to the event.

- **The horse should be lightly exercised** prior to going into the show ring to work off excess energy.

- **Inhand showing classes involve** the horse being led around the ring by a handler. The horse is shown without a saddle.

◀ *The horse needs to become accustomed to the surroundings before the show.*

Mounted games

- **Mounted games are varied** and often include sack, flag, walk-and-trot, egg-and-spoon and bending poles.

- **Games are usually divided** into leading rein races for small children and rider age groups.

- **Rosettes are awarded for first**, second and third places in each event and points are given – the overall champion being awarded a trophy.

- **A good games pony is calm**, but fast-moving and able to stop suddenly.

- **A good gymkhana rider is** well-balanced, stable and able to get on and off a pony easily.

▶ *In the flag race, the rider has to lean over to grab the flag whilst moving and turning at speed.*

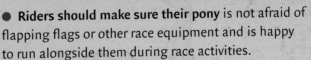

- **Riders should make sure their pony** is not afraid of flapping flags or other race equipment and is happy to run alongside them during race activities.

- **In the UK**, the Pony Club runs a team mounted games competition with the finalists competing at the Horse of the Year Show. The winning team is awarded the Prince Philip Cup.

- **No whips or spurs are allowed in the games**. The rider wears a safety hat, jodhpurs and riding boots. A body protector is optional.

- **The pony should wear** a snaffle bit. Martingales are also allowed.

- **The word gymkhana** comes from India, where mounted games have been played for hundreds of years.

Dressage and showing

● **Dressage allows a horse and rider** to show themselves to be working in harmony.

● **Tests from novice to advanced levels** are carried out in arenas. The horse and rider are judged on how well they execute their movements.

● **Faults during a dressage test** include ignoring the rider's aids, being in the wrong gait and losing impulsion and rhythm.

● **Showing classes are categorized** in many different ways. For example, inhand classes where the horse is led around the ring in front of a judge and ridden classes.

● **The judge pays attention** to how the horse moves, its behaviour, suitability, appearance and conformation.

● **The different classes of showing include:** mountain and moorland for pure bred, British breeds, show hunter, working hunter, cob, and show pony.

▲ An advanced dressage rider, wearing top hat and tails, works at showing the fluidity of the horse's movements.

● **In some ridden show classes**, a judge will ride a horse, as well as watch the animal perform with its rider.

● **In ridden show classes**, riders are required to exhibit horses individually as well as in a group. During this time the judge assesses the behaviour, conformation and paces of the horses.

● **A good showhorse must be obedient** and show no sign of disobeying its rider or displaying any aggression towards other animals.

● **Turn out is all important in showing** and great attention is paid to the detail of mane-plaiting to show off a good head and neck.

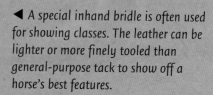

◄ A special inhand bridle is often used for showing classes. The leather can be lighter or more finely tooled than general-purpose tack to show off a horse's best features.

Showjumping

● **Showjumping competitions** are usually restricted to competitors of a certain age, their horse's height or its level of experience.

● **As well as individual jumping competitions**, there are pairs and team events and sometimes even fancy-dress jumping.

● **The competitors are allowed** to walk the course before the competition begins in order to memorize it and work out any tricky stride patterns.

● **A 'fault' is a penalty incurred** if a competitor knocks down or refuses a jump, or exceeds the time allowed.

● **All the riders who manage** a clear round without any faults qualify for a second round of jumping.

● **Upright jumps are straight** up-and-down jumps. Spread jumps are broad jumps with two sets of uprights.

● **A course is set out to include** turns and combination fences, such as double and triples. These are set closer together than other jumps and must be approached at the correct angle and speed.

● **Water jumps may also be included** – either broad troughs of water with a low fence at the front, or a ditch and higher fence.

● **A good showjumping horse** is courageous, quick, agile and athletic, but willing to listen to the rider.

◀ Showjumping takes the form of a course of coloured jumps set out in an arena.

Cross-country and eventing

● **There are different levels** of cross-country, from beginner through to advanced.

● **A horse and rider** have to compete the cross-country course within a set time.

● **Event horses have to be** at least five years old to compete.

● **Competitors are disqualified** if they take the wrong course, fall off twice, or refuse a jump three times.

● **The jumps are spread out** and riders have to pay attention to the condition of the ground to get the best from their horses.

● **As well as individual competitions**, there are team and pairs events.

● **The rider has a chance to walk the course** before competing to study the jumps.

◀ This horse confidently jumps a cross-country fence in water.

● **In horse trials,** competitors take part in dressage, steeplechase, showjumping and cross-country.

● **The dressage test aims to show** that a horse capable of showjumping and cross-country tests is also disciplined and obedient.

● **The road and track sections do not involve jumps**, but test stamina at trot and canter.

Driving

- **Driving was internationally recognized** as a competitive sport in 1969.

- **Driving trials follow a similar format** to ridden three-day events. The competition consists of three phases, using a penalty-scoring system.

- **In Phase A,** competitors have to drive a sequence of set movements. Marks are awarded for obedience, quality of paces and style.

- **Phase B is a marathon over varying distances** – the timed sections have to be completed at different paces.

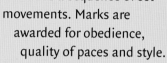

◀ *Blinkers stop the horse becoming frightened by its surroundings.*

★ **STAR FACT** ★
HRH The Duke of Edinburgh has competed a team of Fell Ponies in driving trials.

- **Phase C is an obstacle test** around a course of cones. This phase tests the driver's skill and the obedience of the driving horses.

- **Scurry driving involves driving a pair of ponies** around a mini-obstacle course against the clock.

- **Scurry competitions** are normally divided into two sections: 12 hh and under, and 12 hh to 14.2 hh.

- **Show-ring driving is judged on** the quality of the turnout – horse, vehicle, harness and driver – and style and performance.

- **Large horse shows often have classes** or displays of brewery turnouts.

Endurance riding

- **There are different kinds of endurance ride** – races and non-competitive pleasure or training rides.

- **Rides vary in length** from up to 30 km to over 160 km.

- **Arabs excel at long-distance riding,** cobs and ponies are just as likely to take part on 30 km rides.

- **Before taking part in a ride,** the horse will have a thorough check-up by the vet and the farrier.

- **The welfare of the horse** is very important and competitors can be disqualified on the suggestion of a vet.

- **Along the ride are checkpoints** where riders identify themselves to officials and both the horse and rider are offered a drink.

- **Regular vet checks** are made in longer rides.

★ **STAR FACT** ★
The most well-known long-distance ride in Great Britain is the Golden Horseshoe – a two-day endurance ride over 160 km.

- **On finishing a competitive ride,** the rider has to report back to the vet within a set time to re-present his horse for examination.

- **Rosettes are awarded for completion** of the ride and on the condition of the horse.

- **A horse cannot be younger** than seven years old to take part in more advanced rides.

◀ *Arab horses make excellent endurance horses.*

Western and rodeo

- **The first rodeo** was held in Arizona, USA, in 1866.

- **There are five basic events in a rodeo** – calf roping, steer wrestling, saddle-bronco, bareback and bull riding.

- **There are large money prizes** for event winners, but it is an extremely dangerous sport and injuries are common.

- **In the bucking competitions**, the rider must stay on the animal for ten seconds for saddle-bronco riding and eight seconds for bareback-bronco riding.

- **In calf roping**, riders have to lasso a calf from their horse, tie their rope to the saddle, dismount and tie the calf's legs together.

- **Steer (a young castrated bull) wrestling** involves the rider leaping from his horse to wrestle the steer to the ground.

- **Special cutting horses** are used to separate out steers from a herd. They are skilled at isolating the chosen animal without splitting up the rest of the group.

- **Barrel racing** is a timed competition where horses race around three barrels in a cloverleaf pattern.

- **Reining competitions** are ridden at speed. The horse and rider show co-operation and agility while demonstrating particular movements.

- **The horse is expected** to show quick stops, turns and pivots.

◀ In barrel racing, competetors are penalized for knocking over a barrel.

Polo

- **Polo was introduced to the west** by British cavalry officers serving in India in the 19th century.

- **A fast team game**, polo is now played worldwide.

- **Standard polo involves two teams of four riders** aiming to score goals by hitting a ball through goalposts with a polo stick from horseback.

- **The polo ball** is only 8 cm in diameter. It is usually made from willow root or plastic.

- **The game is split into timed sections** called chukkas which allow the ponies to rest between play.

> ★ STAR FACT ★
> The word polo originates from the Tibetan word pulu meaning ball.

- **A trained polo pony is worth a great deal of money.** It is fast, agile and able to stop instantly from a gallop, and take off again at speed.

- **Polo ponies are taught** to turn at speed and to lean into other ponies.

- **Each rider is allowed to ride** more than one pony in the course of a polo game.

- **Argentina is noted for breeding** quality polo ponies.

◀ Polo ponies have hogged (shaved) manes.

Harness racing

- **Harness racing** is one of the most popular equestrian sports in the world.

- **There are two different gaits** or types of harness-racing horse: the pace horse and the trotting horse.

- **The pace horse, or pacer**, moves its legs in lateral pairs and usually wears special leg hobbles when racing to maintain the pace.

- **The trotting horse** moves its legs in diagonal pairs.

- **If a horse breaks out of the trot pace**, the driver must pull over to the outside of the racetrack, thus losing ground on the other racers.

▶ *Pacers usually wear hobbles to prevent them from breaking their gait.*

- **The horse pulls a sulky,** which is a lightweight two-wheeled vehicle.

- **A mobile starting gate** is used in harness racing to ensure a fair start for all competitors.

- **Harness racing is held on a snow track** at St Moritz in Switzerland. A special sulky sleigh is used to suit the conditions.

- **Horses often wear thick sheepskin nosebands** called shadow rolls. These limit the horses' view of the ground and avoids them shying at shadows.

Olympic Games

- **Three-day eventing and dressage** were introduced to the Olympics in 1912.

- **The first Olympic team** dressage competition was won by Germany in 1928.

- **Riding events are the only competitions** at Olympic level where men and women compete equally.

- **In 1900**, competitions included best equestrian long jump and high jump but these were dropped from the Olympics shortly afterwards.

- **Women were only allowed** to compete in Olympic dressage for the first time in 1952.

- **Liselott Linsenhoff was the first woman to win** gold in an equestrian event as part of the German dressage team, in 1968.

▶ *America, Germany, the Netherlands and Australia won Gold medals at the Olympic Games in Sydney in 2000.*

- **Australian Bill Roycroft** competed for his country with a broken collarbone in 1960 in the three-day team event. They went on to win gold.

- **Lis Hartel of Denmark** won a silver medal in dressage despite being paralyzed by polio in 1944.

- **In 1968**, British rider Jane Bullen was the first woman to win gold in the three-day event.

Other horse sports

- **Drag hunting involves** riders following an artificial scent laid by a human runner.

- **The drag hunt uses hounds to track the scent**, which is laid over open country. The huntsmen and hunt follow, jumping obstacles in their course.

- **Vaulting is gymnastics on a moving horse.** A horse is lunged on a 12 m to 14 m circle by a team member while other members vault on and off the animal.

- **Most vaulting exercises are performed at canter**, although difficult manoeuvres and some fun classes are performed at walk.

- **Horseball** involves leaning right out of the saddle towards the ground to pick up a small football with a strapping harness.

◀ *Drag hunting is an old English tradition.*

- **Horseball is a fast team game** and points are scored by shooting the ball through a hoop.

- **Le Trec is a fast-growing sport** that involves three sections: orienteering, control and an obstacle course.

- **In the obstacle section of Le Trec**, the rider faces hazards that might be met out hacking, for example, opening and closing a gate.

- **Le Trec stands for Technique de Randonnee Equestre de Competition** and originated in France less than 30 years ago.

Preparing to compete

- **Before taking part in any competitive activity**, a horse should be fit, healthy and up to the task.

- **It is up to the rider to ensure that the horse** is fully prepared for the job. This involves assessing its current state of fitness.

- **The tack needs to be checked** for fit and the horse should be shod if necessary.

- **Light work at a walk should be slowly introduced.** It is better to have four or five short sessions throughout a week than two longer workouts.

- **As the horse gains condition**, faster work such as trotting should be introduced and a variety of work should be undertaken, including hacking out and some school work.

- **When it is coping well at canter** and is responsive to the rider's aids, jumping can be reintroduced to the horse's routine.

- **If a gymkhana is the goal**, the pony should be introduced to some of the things it will experience at an event.

- **Home-made flags can be used** to accustom the pony to flags flapping.

- **For dressage competitions** the rider will need to learn the sequence of movements that make up the tests.

- **Regular lessons and training** will improve their skills and help them compete successfully.

▶ *Access to a beach makes fitness training easier. A horse can be exercised on the sand and ridden through the water to cool off.*

Dress codes

● **The traditional attire in showjumping** is a hacking jacket or dark-coloured riding jacket, white or cream jodhpurs, leather boots, a white shirt and a hat in black, brown or navy.

● **Long hair should be worn neatly in a hairnet.** Gloves and body protectors are optional.

● **Black top hat and tails** are only worn for dressage at an advanced level.

● **Jodhpurs or breeches** are pale cream or white and while jodhpur boots can be worn at lower levels, long boots are expected at higher levels.

● **Depending on the type of show class**, the rider is expected to wear a hacking jacket, or black or navy riding jacket, white shirt, cream jodhpurs with brown or black boots and a black or navy hat.

● **Gloves should be black, brown or navy leather.** The tie should not be too bright.

● **The cross-country stage of eventing** allows for greater individuality in what riders can wear. Riders wear a body protector and hard hat, carry a whip and wear spurs.

● **In gymkhanas,** children generally wear cream jodhpurs, a riding hat, jodhpur boots and possibly a body protector. They may wear a white shirt and pony club tie or a sweatshirt.

▼ *The top hat should be worn flat on the head, so that it sits just above the rider's eyebrows.*

● **In western competitions**, riders usually wear a Stetson, a shirt, chaps and leather boots.

● **Endurance riders generally wear** a cross-country or rugby shirt, jodhpurs or riding tights, jodhpur boots or riding trainers, half-chaps, gloves, safety hat. Body protectors are optional.

◀ *A hacking jacket is a tweedlike jacket that is cut to hang neatly while the rider is in the saddle.*

Horses in history

● **The Greek general Xenophon** (427–354 BC) wrote *The Art of Horsemanship*, which is credited with founding modern horsemanship.

● **Roman horsemen were primarily used as messengers.** The Romans protected their horses with body armour while fighting.

▶ Jousting was a fight between two knights on horseback.

● **In tournaments,** knights attempted to defeat an opponent at a variety of competitions.

● **The reins of war horses** were protected by metal plates to prevent the enemy from slicing through them.

● **Knights followed a code of chivalry,** which meant they had to behave honourably.

● **The word chivalry is derived from** the French *cheval*, meaning horse.

● **Heavy horses were used in the Middle Ages** as they were able to support the weight of an armoured knight as well as their own body armour.

● **Stag hunting on horses became popular** in medieval times and the Norman term for starting up a stag became corrupted to the English phrase 'tally-ho'.

● **Chariot racing,** using between two and eight horses, was a popular entertainment in Roman times.

● **Charioteers had to be prepared** to cut themselves free of the reins if a chariot overturned while racing.

Horses in war

● **Horses were important in war** because of their speed and agility.

● **In 330 BC,** the cavalry of Alexander the Great rode over 250 km in only 11 days.

● **The stirrup was an important breakthrough** when it was introduced to western Europe in the 8th century.

● **It meant the rider had greater stability** and could therefore use weapons more effectively.

● **North American Plains Indians** regarded horses as units of currency, and tribes fought over them.

● **The Duke of Wellington rode his favourite horse,** Copenhagen, at the Battle of Waterloo in 1815, when the English defeated the French.

● **Horses were requisitioned in Britain** to support the fighting in World War I.

● **In World War I the cavalry** could not cope with trench warfare, barbed wire or modern artillery and suffered massive casualties.

● **The Trakehner breed from Prussia** was decimated during World War II when the horses were moved from east to west Europe.

● **The numbers of ponies on Dartmoor in England** were much reduced when the army took over the area for training during World War II.

▼ Armour was worn by horse and rider during battle.

Horses at work

- **Horse-drawn mail coaches** began running when roads were improved during the late 18th and early 19th century.

- **From 1815–45** it is estimated that about 150,000 horses were in service in England, pulling mail and stage coaches to transport passengers.

- **After the Industrial Revolution**, horses were used to transport goods into towns, such as pulling rubbish carts.

- **Richard Martin campaigned in England** in the early 1820s for the more humane treatment of horses. They were often overworked, beaten and neglected.

- **The first trams introduced** were horse-drawn and travelled at 9 to 11 km/h.

- **Horses were also used to pull narrow boats** along the canal systems in Britain. They walked along the tow paths beside the canals.

- **Pit ponies were widely used** in the mining industry in Britain until the 1990s in some places.

- **The first cylinder mowers were invented in the 1800s.** They were pulled by horses wearing leather boots to avoid damaging the grass.

- **The pulling power of an engine** is still described in terms of horsepower.

- **One horsepower** is equivalent to 745 Watts.

◀ *This seed drill was designed to be used by horses improve the speed and efficiency of farming.*

Horses in public service

- **Mounted police are used worldwide** – the most famous are the Royal Canadian Mounted Police (RCMP).

- **The RCMP's role is largely ceremonial today.** Their horses are black, heavy Thoroughbred types and stand about 16 hh to 17 hh.

- **The Mounties created a musical ride** to show off their considerable riding ability and to entertain the public.

▼ *The Mounties' musical ride is a series of movements ridden at speed.*

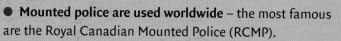

> ★ **STAR FACT** ★
> The last US army horse died in 1976 aged 29. He was called Black Jack.

- **One of their formations** called the 'dome' was featured on a 50 dollar Canadian bill.

- **Each year**, foals born in the Mounties' stables have names beginning with the same letter.

- **The first mounted police force in Britain** was the London Bow Street Horse Patrol in 1760.

- **Police horses are trained to ignore missiles**, crowds and sudden noise and learn how to step over obstacles thrown in their path.

- **Police horses provide support** to the rest of the police force.

- **In England**, the Thames Valley Police Mounted Section patrol royal and parliamentary occasions.

Horses in literature

● **The highwayman Dick Turpin rode** a mare called Black Bess.

● **In Robert Burns' poem *Tam o' Shanter*,** a drunk Tam has to place his faith in his horse Meg to help him flee from angry witches.

● **Shakespeare's *Richard III*** has the well-known line 'A horse, a horse, my kingdom for a horse'.

● **The poem *The Charge of the Light Brigade*** by Lord Tennyson commemorates the Battle of Balaclava during the Crimean War in 1854.

● **The Trojan Horse** was built by the ancient Greeks as a gift for the Trojans. The Greeks hid inside it, crept out at night, and defeated the Trojans.

● **Don Quixote de la Mancha** was the creation of the panish poet Miguel de Cervantes in the 17th century. He rode a horse called Rosinante and was accompanied on his travels by his friend Sancho Panza.

● **In Jonathan Swift's *Gulliver's Travels*,** written in 1726, creatures called houyhnhnms appear. They were talking horses.

● **The Pullein-Thompson sisters** were prolific writers of horse and pony books for children. They began writing in the 1940s while still in their teens.

◀ *The Trojan horse was an enormous wooden horse built by the ancient Greeks during the Trojan Wars.*

Women and horses

● **Lady Isobel Blunt** (1837–1917), together with her husband, set up an Arab stud in Egypt.

● **Calamity Jane** (1852–1903) toured the US in Wild West shows and was skilled at riding and shooting.

● **Mrs Christian Davies** (1667–1739) rode through Flanders disguised as a man in search of her husband who was fighting in battle.

● **Emily Davison** (1872–1913) was a suffragette who was killed when she tried to catch hold of the king's horse during the Derby races.

● **Alicia Meynell** was the first female jockey to ride in an official horse race in 1804.

● **Annie Oakley** (1860–1926) was an American rodeo star and sharp shooter who appeared in Buffalo Bill's Wild West Touring Show.

● **Lucinda Prior-Palmer** was an outstanding event rider. She won the prestigious Badminton Horse Trials six times between 1973 and 1984.

● **Pat Smythe** (1928–96) was Britain's first Olympic woman rider and the most successful female showjumper of her time.

▶ *Annie Oakley was famed for her accurate shooting – even when moving at speed on horseback.*

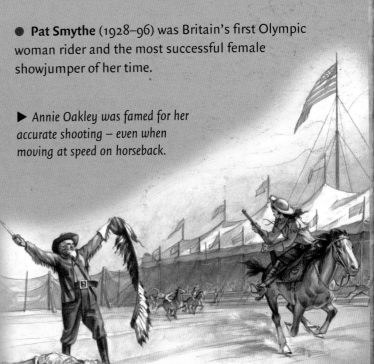

Horses in the spotlight

▶ Black Beauty is a famous fictional horse.

● **In the 1944 film *National Velvet*,** Velvet Brown rides her horse to victory in the Grand National, but is later disqualified when officials discover she is a girl.

● **Anna Sewell's 1877 novel,** ***Black Beauty*,** tells the story of a horse and his companions and was made into a film starring Sean Bean in 1994.

● ***On White Horses* was the theme tune** to a popular children's television programme in the 1960s. The show featured Lipizzaner horses that were trained at a stud farm.

● **Gene Autrey was a famous singing cowboy** during the 1930s, 40s and 50s. He featured in many film stunts with his horse Champion.

● **Norman Thelwell** (1923–2004) created cartoons of round, fat ponies and child riders in amusing situations.

● **Roy Rogers and his horse Trigger** performed many publicity stunts, such as signing into hotels using a pencil held between Trigger's teeth.

● **In the 1998 film, *The Horse Whisperer*,** Robert Redford's character treats a horse that has been badly traumatized in an accident.

● **Buffalo Bill Cody** featured a horse called Sultan in his Wild West shows in the 1880s.

● **Mr Ed the 'Talking Horse',** was a much loved 'talking' palomino who appeared in a 1960s television series.

● **Shadowfax, the greatest of the horses of Rohan**, was Gandalf's horse in Tolkien's Lord of the Rings.

The Wild West

▶ Cowboys wore chaps over their trousers to protect their legs while riding.

● **The Plains Indians** branded their horses with identifying marks to signify which horses belonged to which tribe.

● **Horses were important** to North American Indians for hunting.

● **The Shishoni Indians** hung precious objects around their horses' necks to protect them in battle.

● **A cowboy's most prized possession** was his saddle. Even if he gambled everything else away including his horse, he would retain the saddle and carry it on his back.

● **The Sioux Indians** painted horses on their tepees and made halters and ropes out of horsehair and buffalo hide.

● **The Crow Indians** were famed for their horse skills – both as horse whisperers and as exceptional riders.

★ STAR FACT ★
Indian warriors painted their horses for protection and courage. The symbols could be simple hand prints, stripes or animal designs.

● **Wild Bill Hickok**, was born in 1812 in Illinois, USA. A gunman and a sheriff, he also acted as a scout for the US cavalry. He was killed by a bullet in the back during a card game in 1876.

● **The Pony Express mail service** began in 1860, travelling between St Joseph, Missouri to San Francisco. Within two years the service was replaced by stage coaches.

● **Gauchos of Argentina** are the South American equivalent of the North American cowboy. Skilled horsemen, it is said that if a gaucho is without a horse he is without legs.

Myths and legends

- **The four horsemen of the Apocalypse**; Conquest, Famine, Plague and War are said to signify the end of the world. They represent the four evils of the world.

- **Pegasus**, the winged horse in Greek mythology, carried Zeus' thunderbolt.

- **In Norse mythology**, Odin the god of war had an eight-legged horse called Sleipnir who could travel across the sky and sea.

- **A unicorn is a mythical beast** that has the body of a pure white horse with a twisted horn on its head. It symbolizes good and purity.

- **According to Arabian legend**, the god Allah created the Arab horse 'out of a handful of the southern wind'.

▶ *The horn of the unicorn was believed to have magical powers.*

★ STAR FACT ★
In Roman times, white horses were a symbol of the gods and power.

- **In Irish mythology**, the horse was believed to carry souls of the dead from this world to the next.

- **Poseidon, the Greek god of the sea**, rode a chariot drawn by half-horse half-fish creatures.

- **Kelpies feature in Scottish mythology**. They attract people towards water by appearing as beautiful women then drag their victim underwater while taking on the form of a water horse.

- **In Greek mythology**, the gods of the sun and moon rode chariots across the sky each dawn and dusk.

Horses in art

- **Cave paintings of horses** from around 15000 BC have been found in Europe.

- **Pictish stone carvings** of sea horses from AD 400–700 still stand in Scotland.

- **Sculptures of horses** and bronze chariots were buried in the tomb of the first Chinese emperor more than 2000 years ago.

- **Rosa Bonheur** (1832–99) was a French painter who specialized in horses. She painted the famous *Horse Fair* in 1853.

- **Theodore Gericault** (1791–1824) was a keen horseman and painter. Tragically the French artist died as a result of a horse riding accident.

- **George Stubbs** (1724–1806) was a popular English painter who made a study of the anatomy of horses and published a book called *The Anatomy of the Horse* in 1766.

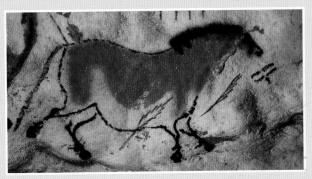

◀ *Early cave paintings were drawn using earth or carbon mixed with water or animal fat.*

- **Leonardo da Vinci** (1452–1519) made detailed anatomical drawings of horses.

- **The Flemish painter** Anthony Van Dyck (1599–1641) depicted Charles I on horseback in 1637–38.

- **Russian-born Vassily Kandinsky** (1866–1944) and the German Franz Marc (1880–1916) founded a group of artists in 1911 called *Der Blaue Reiter* (The Blue Rider).

- **Elizabeth Frink** (1930–93) was an English sculptor whose early work included a series of horse and rider sculptures.

Horse folklore

- **Horseshoes are often fixed onto buildings** and stable doors as they are thought to bring good luck.

- **A myth exists that Lady Godiva rode naked** through the town of Coventry, England in the 11th century, on a grey horse to protest at taxes.

- *Ride a Cock-horse* **is** a traditional English folk rhyme. It is believed to relate to Queen Elizabeth I of England and tells the story of how she travelled to the town of Banbury.

- **Rutland Castle in England** has a tradition where visiting lords have to present a horseshoe to the castle.

- **Horses brasses**, metal ornaments that are attached to heavy agricultural horse harnesses, are often considered to be lucky.

- **Giant white horses** are carved in chalk on some hillsides in England, some dating back hundreds of years.

- **Folklore stories** say that when King Arthur of the Round Table returns to the throne one of the chalk horses will get up and dance.

- **An Irish folk cure** for toothache suggests rubbing the affected area of the jaw with a dead horse's tooth to relieve the pain.

- **According to Arabian folklore**, the chestnut horse is the fastest and bravest of all horses.

- **In Celtic folklore** it is said to be bad luck to cross the path of ploughing horses.

◄ *Horseshoes have traditionally been the symbol of good luck.*

Famous horses

- **Man o' War was a famous US racehorse** who began racing in 1919. He won 20 out of 21 races.

- **According to the historian Plutarch**, Alexander the Great tamed his horse Bucephalus.

- **Foxhunter was a 16.3 hh showjumper** ridden by Sir Harry Llewellyn, and they won an Olympic medal for Great Britain.

- **Red Rum won the Grand National** three times in the 1970s. He died at the age of 30 and is buried at Aintree race course.

- **Arkle is described as** the greatest steeplechaser ever. He raced during the 1960s and died in 1970.

▶ *Bucephalus was Alexander the Great's horse that he rode for thousands of miles and into many battles.*

> ★ **STAR FACT** ★
> In 1947, the funeral of the racehorse Man o' War was attended by 2000 people.

- **Shergar**, a famous racehorse in the 1980s was kidnapped from a stud in Ireland in 1983. Never recovered, his disappearance remains a mystery.

- **Stroller was a 14.2-hh pony** ridden by British rider Marion Coakes in the 1968 Olympic Games. He was the only pony to have competed at this level and they won the silver medal.

- **Comanche was the only US cavalry horse** to survive the Battle of Little Bighorn or Custer's Last Stand in 1876. Comanche was injured but recovered from his wounds and became a national hero.

Royal riders

● **Queen Boudicca of the Iceni**, famous for leading an uprising against the Romans in England around AD 60, was a keen horse breeder. It is believed that she exported some horses to Rome.

● **King Alexander III of Scotland** died in 1286 when he rode his horse over a cliff in Fife during the night.

● **Princess Anne of Bohemia** is credited with making the side saddle popular in England after she married Richard II in 1381.

● **Henry VIII** (1497–1543) was presented with Burgundian horse armour that covered the horse's neck, face and body by the Holy Roman Emperor Maximilian I around 1510.

● **A keen horseman in his youth**, Henry VIII is said to have tired out up to ten horses while out hunting for the day. He suffered a permanently damaged leg at the age of 44 when a horse rolled over on him at a tournament.

● **Henry VIII's daughter Elizabeth I**, was said to have been a very able horsewoman who rode faster than her male contemporaries.

● **After the death of Oliver Cromwell**, Charles II returned to England in 1660 and reinstated horse racing, which had been banned. He even took part in races himself under the alias 'Old Rowley'.

● **Queen Elizabeth II** has been an able horsewoman since childhood and has an active interest in horse racing. Her husband, HRH The Duke of Edinburgh, has also been a keen polo player and competed in driving competitions.

● **Princess Anne**, the Princess Royal, took part in the three-day team event for Britain in the Olympics of 1976.

▲ Queen Elizabeth II has attended the Trooping the Colour ceremony every year since the start of her reign in 1952.

▶ Boudicca was a keen horsewoman. This shows her standing aboard a horse-drawn chariot.

Horse trivia

- **A horse's knee joint** is equivalent to a human wrist and its hock joint, the ankle.

- **A horse wearing a green ribbon** on its tail is young and inexperienced. A red ribbon is a warning to other riders that the horse might kick out.

- **The largest horse museum** in the world is the International Museum of the Horse in Lexington, Kentucky, USA.

◀ *Competition horses can be taught to tackle obstacles they would naturally avoid.*

★ STAR FACT ★
A horse's heart weighs about 4 kg.

- **As a horse ages** the hollows above its eyes become more prominent.

- **A 16-year-old horse** is about 50 years old in human terms. Ponies generally live longer – sometimes well into their 50s.

- **The average length of a horse's stride** at walk is 1.67 m to 1.83 m.

- **A horse has approximately** 18 m of small intestine and 6 m of large intestine.

- **Normal horse droppings** are at least 15 percent water.

- **Horses can detect** both higher and lower sound ranges than humans.

Body talk

- **The normal temperature** for a horse at rest is 38.3°C to 38.6°C.

- **A horse can see a moving object clearly**, but has difficulty determining the distance between objects.

- **It is not clear from research** which colours a horse can see.

- **A horse can sleep standing up** because of a locking mechanism in its leg.

- **There are about one million horses** in the UK today.

- **To find a horse's rug size**, a measurement is taken from the mid point of its chest to the edge of its flanks.

- **On average**, a horse has drowsy periods that total between two and four hours a day.

- **An ergot is a small horny growth** found at the back of a horse's fetlock join.

- **Grass sickness** is a disease affecting the nerves controlling a horse's gut. It can be fatal.

★ STAR FACT ★
In warm countries, horses are said to enjoy oranges, grapefruits and dates.

▼ *A well-fitted rug should fit snugly around the neck, while allowing for plenty of shoulder movement.*

Facts and figures

● **At the peak period of feeding**, a nursing mare can produce up to 18 l of milk per day.

● **A horse uses about 80 percent** of the energy gained from food in keeping warm.

● **Horses generally find it soothing** to have their ears gently rubbed.

● **Horses have seven common blood types** and can be used as blood donors for other horses. There is a blood bank in Falkirk, Scotland.

● **Horses' bodies** consist of 65 percent water.

◀ These mares and foals are enjoying cantering around their paddock.

● **Horses produce** up to 10 l of urine daily.

● **To check if a horse is hydrated**, press the gum above an incisor until it becomes pale. The area should should turn pink again one to two seconds if the animal is healthy and hydrated.

● **The length of a horse's stride** is measured between two successive imprints of the same foot.

● **Cantering** is a three-speed gait: 1–2–3, 1–2–3.

Terminology

● **Napping is when the horse or pony** refuses to do what its rider asks.

● **The bit is the mouthpiece**, usually made of metal, which is placed in a horse's mouth.

● **A martingale is an item of tack** that is designed to prevent the horse raising its head too high.

● **A breastplate** stops a saddle slipping backwards.

● **The horn and cantle** are the highest points at the front and back of a western saddle.

● **A livery or a boarding stable** is a stable yard where horseowners pay a professional to look after their horses, on a full-time or part-time basis.

● **A hack is a ride out** that should be enjoyable for both horse and rider.

● **A menage is an arena** that is used for riding and schooling horses.

● **Bots are flies** that lay eggs on a horse's skin.

● **Metal bits were first used** for horses between 1300 and 1200 BC.

◀ A numnah or saddle cloth, is usually placed underneath a saddle to provide extra comfort for the horse's back.

Horse talk

- **Cast describes a horseshoe** that is lost or comes off accidentally. It can also refer to a horse that gets stuck while lying down.

- **To change the rein** means to change direction.

- **A lasso is a long rope** with a loop at the end used to catch cattle and other animals.

- **A saddle-rack** is a wooden or metal support on which a saddle is stored when not being used.

- **A pressure halter** teaches a horse not to pull away from its handler, by applying pressure to the nose and poll area.

- **Poles are used in a variety of ways** to train horses to be aware of their bodies and feet.

- **Quarter marks are used to show off** the good condition of a show horse's coat. They can be applied by using special plastic stencil sheets or by using a fine comb.

- **Spooky is used to describe a horse** that is liable to shy or start away from an object that is unfamiliar or frightening.

- **Turn out describes the area** where a horse is grazed and allowed to move about freely.

- **Warbles are caused** by warble flies that lay eggs on a horse's coat. The larvae penetrate the skin to make painful lumps.

◀ Horses enjoy the freedom of being turned out in a field.

Equine terms

- **Irons are another name** for stirrups.

- **Electrolytes are minerals and salts** found in the horse's body. Supplements can be given to a horse to help replace those lost from excess sweating.

- **Forage is the term for bulk food**, such as hay or grass, and should form the basis for all equine feeding programmes.

- **Ad lib is a term often used in relation to forage.** It means that forage is always available to the horse and it is not rationed.

- **Schooling is the term used when** a horse is being trained to learn and obey specific commands called aids.

- **A schoolmaster is a horse that is calm** and obedient and will obey commands correctly.

- **Gait is another word for pace.** A horse usually has four basic gaits: walk, trot, canter and gallop.

- **The 'inside leg'** refers to whichever leg is nearest the centre of a circle when a horse is being schooled in a ring.

- **Branding** is a method of permanently marking a horse, so that it can be identified.

- **Haw is the word for a horse's third eyelid.** It is a thin membrane of skin that can be drawn over the eye.

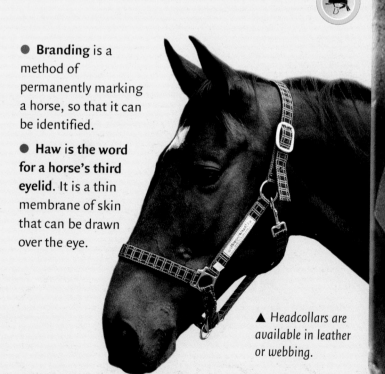

▲ Headcollars are available in leather or webbing.

Horse loves

● **Horses enjoy being able to pick** at food over a long period of time.

● **Horses who get along** will stand grooming each other, nibbling the skin at the base of each other's withers.

● **Rolling on the ground** after exercise is pleasurable to a horse.

● **Horses enjoy routine.** They like to be fed at regular times and to be kept near familiar companions.

● **The freedom to graze** and roam around at will is enjoyed by horses.

● **Horses love company –** preferably that of other horses.

● **Horses often like a bath** if the weather is really hot. They can be sponged and hosed down to cool them off.

● **Horses prefer the familiar** and may be reluctant to try a new route or ride out on their own if they are used to being ridden in company.

● **Scratching up against trees** or stable walls is enjoyed by most horses.

● **Horses usually prefer** to be stroked rather than patted.

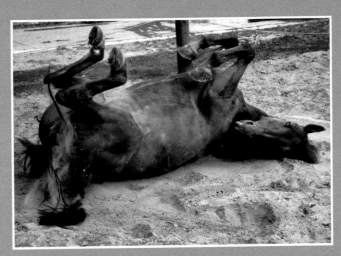

◄ Horses enjoy rolling, which helps improve circulation and skin condition.

Horse hates

● **Horses hate to be tied up so tightly** that they cannot move their heads or look around.

● **Stones in a horse's feet may cause discomfort.** Small stones and sharp twigs can puncture the hoof sole and create abscesses and lameness.

● **Being startled or approached quickly from behind** may cause a horse to kick out. Any unexpected incident or occurence may cause a horse to spook or react in an unpredictable way.

◄ A horse's first reaction to danger is to flee.

● **Horses will become bored** if left for lengthy periods of time in a stable. This may cause behavioural problems.

● **Horses do not enjoy continuous rain.** If their coat becomes soaked through, they may develop sores on their skin.

● **Horses hate** to be chased.

● **Ill-fitting tack will cause a horse distress.** Regular checks should be made to ensure it is not causing any discomfort to the horse.

● **Horses dislike riders** who pull on their mouths and are unbalanced in the saddle.

● **Mares will become distressed** if separated from their foals. They will repeatedly call for them if weaning is carried out unsympathetically.

★ STAR FACT ★
Many horses are said to be frightened of pigs.

INDEX